Puff Adders in the Panicum

Andrew Hutchinson

Published by Andrew Hutchinson, 2023.

PUFF ADDERS IN THE PANICUM

First edition. January 11, 2023.

ISBN: 978-0639708577

Written by Andrew Hutchinson.

Table of Contents

Foreword

A puff adder is a slow moving adder with a robust girth, massive cerebral structure and overly long fangs. This serpent uses its muscular ability and impressive orthodontics to deliver multiple strikes with extreme speed. The puff adder is a master of disguise, blending into its surroundings, lying in wait to ambush unsuspecting prey ... its toxins attacking tissue and making it rotten that which was fit and functioning. Panicum is a particularly sweet pasture grass, excellent for fattening livestock. Panicum is an apt parallel in the description of the Eastern Cape. Offerings of sweet success and the promise of prosperity are real - however, beware the puff adders in the panicum ... "As once told to me by Twitch."

Acknowledgements

To all the memory makers, supporters and members of the animal kingdom!

With thanks to ...

Cally for all the cups of coffee

Mikayla for all the food

My Kirst for all the love!

And to you!

Glossary & terms

<u>Foreword</u>

Panicum – a type of pasture grass.

Arietans (striking violently)

Cicada – a manufactured brand of air rifle

Kwedins – young AmaXhosa boys

Bitis Arietans – scientific name for puff adder

Manley Flats

AmaXhosa – African tribe encountered by the 1820 settlers in the

Eastern Cape region of South Africa

Nguni/Sanga – an African breed of cattle. Nguni cattle are a principal form of Sanga cattle – a collective name for indigenous cattle of sub-Saharan Africa

Queenstown Catastrophe

Tollies – young castrated bull calves

Zol – rolled marijuana cigarette

Ganga – marijuana

Pig stories

Digitaria – indigenous grass species

Cowboys on the Collective

Blesbok – an antelope with a blaze of white down the forehead

Translations

The Colonel

Dink jy dis 'n fokkin vlieg wat verby gaan?

(Do you think it's a fucking fly going by?

Manley Flats

Kraal – livestock holding facility

Plakkies – slipslops/ sandals

Grensvegter – border fighter – a reference to South African army type, usually connected to the Angolan Border War. "Krokodil" – crocodile

Introduction to Plakkies

Fudu – water terrapin

Plakkies continued

"Engelsman waars jou geld?" – "Englishman where is your money?"

Gawie Grootbaard – Gawie Big Beard – surname

Lewendehawe – livestock

Queenstown Catastrophe

Stoep – porch

Standerton

"Hulle is leeg manne." – "They are empty, men."

Mercy mercy

Spekboom – a round leafed succulent plant

Skelm – wily /clever

Valkyrie – a Nordic angel of death

Kloof – valley

House of Orange

Kak – shit

Koppies – low rounded hills

Comrade

Hier kom kak – here comes shit

Oubaas – the old boss or old man

Boet 'n swaer – brother and brother-in-law

Yodwa – alone

Ticks 'n Things

Maplotters – plot dwellers – owners of small pieces of ground

The dart

Sosatie – skewer of meat

Error of Judgement

Poes –vulgar description of female reproductive organ/vagina

01

ARIETANS
(STRIKING VIOLENTLY)

The Harvest Vale farmhouse sits brooding over the hazy, hot Bushman's River Valley. Not a breeze to speak of - still air stifles any kind of relief. The colours of mixed shale, clay, Eastern Cape thicket and the far off red cliff mutate in the shimmer of the afternoon oven. This valley was pretty central to my growth as a pubescent youngster, participating in bushbuck hunting, prawn netting, paddling my surfboard down to the mouth of this snaking, salty waterway ... and the shack! The shack was a construction of packing case material and timber decking set on support poles, amongst the thorn trees. Nestled into the big acacias just up from the private jetty, this was a very special hidey-hole! I loved it there.

Many adventures were had in and around the Bushman's River and a plethora of images remain in my memory bank. During the 'bush boy' childhood in this carved out landscape, there were hardships and near misses that would shape and mould my understanding of the world about me. Apart from the illness contracted from consuming a vast number of prawns from a netting expedition and a few other close shaves, there is one instance that will stick with me forever.

The afternoon oven is relentless, the dry heat making me a little lethargic and somewhat slow. Plinking cans in the rockery of the front garden help pass the time. The bougainvillaea petals are strewn about in abundance, the pretty, purple lantern shaped flowers are dried out and sprinkle the uneven stone paving with a tint of beauty. Underneath the dabs of purple, the stones are warm with heat trapped from the morning sun.

Bullseye! The marksman's lead pellet strikes the tin can, knocking the tin target into a backflip off the rockery perch. The Cicada pellet gun had spoken. I loved that air rifle! The break barrel action was smooth and the open V-sights came up, well balanced, with the butt fitting snugly in my shoulder. Mice, rats, mouse birds, doves, starlings and the odd rabbit came under fire when the kwedins and I 'hunted and gathered' in the kloof. On this afternoon, the Cicada would stave off a life-changing, hemotoxic hell!

Birds in the bushveld are great indicators and forewarning systems. Failure to pay attention to scattering flocks of birds or alarm calls can be expensive in terms of your physical health or even your living presence on this planet.

Sometimes, these messengers require an eye that looks into the shadows, an eye that filters the light, a trained eye that will realise one, the gift of chance ... Eastern Cape thicket has a large footprint of shadow and a canopy of half-light. Hunting bushbuck hones the eye and gives the gift of shadow dancing - much like speed reading. Your eye gathers the important shapes, interprets the information and feeds data to the brain.

My gift on this lethargic, heat-filled afternoon came in the form of a Cape Robin. Not understanding the significance of the statuesque bird in my close proximity nearly cost me dearly. A Cape Robin is not an LBJ (Little Brown Job) of a bird. This chap always has his chest puffed out and scoots around the garden with confidence and a sense of station. A Sergeant Major amongst the hoppers.

As I take aim at another hapless tin can, trigger finger ready for the squeeze, my closing left eye filters the bird's body shape in the twisted, thrusting bark of the bougainvillaea. My right eye seeks out the V sight atop the Cicada barrel but my left eye won't close and shut out the Cape Robin! This Rufus rascal stands absolutely rigid! A Madame Toussade figurine!

The processing starts ... How did this bird suddenly appear? Why is it not moving? Why is it not bothered by my presence? Is it trying to tell me something ...?

I've held my shooting position, while my left eye searches for clues as to the bird's message. I focus both eyes on the task now. A real sense of foreboding creeps up my spine out of my numb bum. The leaf litter and bougainvillaea clutter forces the acquired visual skill to the fore! My visual abilities pierce

the shadow shelf underneath the dried, upturned debris. A tingle and a jangle of nerve endings sees the hairs on my arms raise themselves in a perpendicular angle and my body is somewhat stricken. The bird remains stoic and unmoving.

A flicker of black followed by a thin forked sliver of black, slowly tests the abstract space created by the randomly fallen leaf pile.

The nostrils and the eye pockets piece together the huge tyre tracked patterns on the scales of the boulder-size head. This is the biggest puff adder I have ever seen! My vision includes the bird, the snake, the dead, brown leaves and the spent bougainvillaea lanterns ... and not much else! It is all immediate and close.

Stress hormones flood my system resulting in a slack jaw and vacant mind! I have no plans. My left leg begins trembling, involuntarily and my toes twitch. The amplified silence masks my scream of terror as the giant serpent's cerebral mass moves to strike! The lightning quick poise dislodges the leaf litter sending dry matter asunder to reveal the master of disguise - *Bitis arietans* - a puff adder.

My bare foot is not two feet away from the lips of the S-poised serpent. The parted upper and lower jaws hint at the silky white interior of the puff adder's maw. The lips part further from each other and the angle of the head changes. The bird gets airborne with a wing assisted hop and it's gone. This snake is flexing its hypodermic fangs, flaring them forward. A full, whitenoise of warning escapes from the adder's nostrils. This viper possesses limited ability to modify the acoustics of its exhalant airstream. It is a basic, primal, 'shit yourself' sound!

Flight mode kicks in and the loaded air rifle clatters down on the stoep's steps. It's a mad scramble backwards on all fours - in reverse! I make it across the threshold of the open front door. The Cicada is discarded, left lying, loaded on the steps. A moist palm print spoor upon the hot, red paint of the porch marks my retreat. Peering out from the dusky interior of the house, I cannot see the scales, but the wide body trail excavated amongst the leaves indicate a hasty change of position for the puff adder.

Decision time! Get the Cicada or close the door ... it's 'get the gun!' My fingers grip the butt and hoist it upwards, grabbing the stock with my left hand; I walk backwards towards the doorway. The massive head lifts above the last step, tongue flicking while the balance of the fat adder propels the business end towards me. I shoot from the hip, the pellet ricochets off the porch, striking just next to the puff adder's flexing neck muscles. It pauses, testing the surface of the red paint, tasting the moisture of my palm print!

Spilling the pellets from the Marksman box, I select one with a shaking thumb and forefinger. Left-hand breaks the barrel, right hand pushes the pellet unevenly into the barrel's aperture. *SNAP*! The lever system closes the barrel and the spring is compressed! The Cicada hairpin trigger awaits my fingertip touch. Still the puff adder advances! Tshweeee - the pellet flies off the porch, marking the red paint. *Bitis arietans* stops and decides to present me with a side view of its impressive girth and snub-nosed head. The head is grotesque in size! "It's time to realise my gift of chance!"

The first pellet smacks the snake on the hinge of the jaw. At this range the full-feet-per-second muzzle velocity breaks the jawbone and whips the viper's head around in a whiplash of concentrated energy! The fat tube of muscle follows the impact-affected head. Twisting and turning through the air, the puff adder flashes yellow-black, yellow coloured scales as the cylinder shaped body gymnasts over the descending steps. The hypodermic fangs are reaching out, desperate for a strike, looking for the surface tension that will allow the flow of venom! It finds nought! But another well-placed pellet to the back end of the skull is released. Wild thrashing about causes leaves to float upward and resettle over the twisting, turning serpent.

Break barrel, load, aim, squeeze - I finish the remaining pellets that are scattered about on the wooden floor. Eventually the writhing comes only from confused nerve endings within the reptile's frame. I sink to the floor, sitting cross-legged on the wooden floor beams – shaking, alone at home ...

I was thirteen and had just had my first proper encounter with a puff adder.

02

THE COLONEL

It's 2008 and the world markets go into a spin and self-destruct ... confidence in the South African situation beats a hasty retreat and with that the farm sales market dries up overnight. The crocodile of life keeps coming and I need another plan.

I make my acquaintance with the Colonel and shortly I am sitting in a lecture room with twelve other 'hopefuls'. We all want to be successful and graduate from the South African College of Auctioneering. A couple of the wannabes haven't paid their fees over to the Colonel and he's not starting the course before everyone has crossed his palm ... the last of the hopefuls pays the Colonel and we are prepared for our new journey into the world of the auctioneer's chant and the art of financial extraction. The Colonel takes up his position of authority in the front of the room, clears his throat and casually announces that he has trained in excess of ten thousand aspirant auctioneers but only one per cent of those are operators ... at this, I realise that everyone currently sitting in the room is exempt and that the Colonel has sold hope to all of us ... but statistically none of us should make it. By nine a.m. the first student 'rings the bell'. The Colonel knows how to work the room and I would say that by the end of the first day he knew who had paid him for nothing and who had a real shot at not only graduating from the college but actually going on to calling bids and serving their community. The first evening after class the Colonel invites all of us to the pub -

this proves to be another unaudited section of the learning curve. The following morning, only two students show up on time. Ten students unwittingly eliminated themselves from the course and faded into obscurity. The chap from Otjiwarongo and I now had the respect and attention of the Colonel. We practise the 'chant', we study legal issues and we draw down on years of experience from the Colonel. The final day of the course arrives and we head off to the stock sales yard.

The Colonel has arranged for a few of his students to take to the podium and conduct a few lots of live cattle sales. On the way to the stockyard, the chaps in my vehicle produce a bottle of Vodka and offer a little "Dutch courage," I politely refuse. The stock sales pit is gloomy, dank and reeks of bovine excrement and urine mixed in with human body odour and exhaled nicotine. I take my place on the podium and the first lot is ushered in. A mild panic sets in and I realise this isn't a dummy run. I'm not sure of the market price per kg of these beasts and I start the bid way above the going rate ... the hardened buyers smell blood and wait until my bid is almost 'rock bottom'. Eventually one of the 'stock thieves' gestures with his right hand - moving in rapid circles, much like a Gymnogene (bird of prey) prehensile claw. I am so surprised,

I ask: "Is that a bid sir?" The reply comes at speed, accompanied by a terse form of irritation - Afrikaans in the spoken form is not universal and is so very apt in its application, to those fluent in it - "Dink jy dis 'n fokkin vlieg wat verby gaan?" The buyers crowed and I made him pay for the lot, while he sat revelling in these bully tactics. That chap taught me more in thirty seconds than I had learned the whole week.

03

MANLEY FLATS

Manley Flats, a stronghold of settler sentiment and that age old ethos - take root and thrive ... or perish! It seemed fitting that I would establish a foothold in the livestock and auctioneering world, here, at this bastion of tenacity and determination. Adjacent and east of Manley Flats is the Coombs - a long rectangular basin stretching towards the Fish River mouth. The Coombs bore the brunt of many amaXhosa raiding parties yet was also home to the likes of Edward Driver. Drivers Bush farm, at the top end of the Coombs, was his base from where he traded in the Great Fish River Valley. I came to own Drivers Bush and would often look out over the Fish River Valley, wondering about the clash of humanity that this ribbon of water was charged with keeping separate. "Imagine the trading, the fighting, and the envy from both sides and all the while, the timeless herds of cattle."

AmaXhosa raiding parties would easily ford the river and the follow-up regimental reprisals were twofold in purpose - retribution most definitely, whilst cattle rustling made the military effort worthwhile.

These cattle bore no resemblance to the breeds from Europe.

These cattle were agile, could climb steep slopes, and they were capable of being driven over distance. They were a pure African breed that carried their ID numbers on their hides - each hide like a finger print – a stamp of origin - Nguni /Sanga!

15

I approached the Manley Flats farmers' association and shortly the abandoned auction pens were resurrected and we held sales under a great tent - much like P. T. Barnum, I had brought the greatest show. The farmers' association and the cricket club benefitted from our monthly auctions and enjoyed newfound life.

Nguni type cattle were not in demand by feedlots and had a low commercial value. I saw this breed from another perspective.

Manley Flats had easy access to the historical homelands and pastures of the amaXhosa and the 'kraals of time'.

Homesteads in this region supplied the Witwatersrand with underground migrant labour. Money from the 'reef' found its way back to the families and their living banks - the cattle. Oxen were a valuable trade commodity against replacement heifers - we traded, bought and sold animals to and from these communities. Idutywa, Mgazana and rural Peddie were rich trade reservoirs.

At the time, commercial farmers were concentrating on Stud

Book cattle and unregistered or Nguni type cattle struggled for good prices on auctions across the country. Manley Flats became a showcase for Nguni type cattle as I marketed and boosted the breed.

The first Nguni type cattle sale at Manley's enjoyed great support. Traders fought 'tooth and nail' with wild bids and the meat buyers that arrived, expecting to score cheap cattle off punctured propaganda, got the shock of their lives. 'The Scarlet Pimpernel' suitably attired, sporting a red shawl and matching beret, commanded the rank and file buyers like a boss! He punished each likely bidder with casual confidence reeling in the best lots of the day. I used him on many lots as a benchmark bidder - this frustrated the bejesus out of 'Krokodil'. I let the meat buyers grab a few opening lots as they had to fill transport trucks! On this day, between 'Plakkies', 'Pimpernel' and the 'Grensvegter', the 'beef boys' had a torrid time. On one parcel of bull calves, Krokodil snapped and threw his chair out of the tent – Pimpernel's finger signalled two on top!! A double increment bid and yelled "Tricks, tricks," while I toted the gavel and machine gunned the numbers! 'Obelix' was 'yiiiip, yiiip' next to me, as the backbencher bids simulated sidewinder missiles coming at us from across the ring!

What a sale it was! Manley's was on the map!

Manley Flats expanded into small stock and loose goods, something for everyone!

Manley Flats Auction had no scale to weigh cattle; we were an old school trader's affair under the massive old fig trees and the tent, having the time of our lives. The auctions consolidated and space became an issue. We needed a second venue. I built an auction facility from scratch at the Seven Fountains Sports Club and we ran two monthly sales. I found a financier in an old Graeme College acquaintance and swelled the auctions with 'red' calves. Parcels of beef bullocks lured the likes of Krokodil and 'The Officer' back to our sales. Perception is everything and with the notion of commercial success, so came the added support. Manley Flats was becoming a thorn in the side for 'the other guys'.

Settler family trees and the old school tie bond these Albany folk inextricably together. They are all cousins or joined by marriage or money - the latter being rather important if you happen to be a 'price taking' farmer in between a wool cheque or calving seasons. I began to discover how ingratiated 'the other guys' had become in these farmers' lives. Irrigation system loans, fertilisers and taking care of medical bills in some instances. All the farmers' associations received financial benefit from the scale at the Grahamstown stock sale. When you take all of the above into consideration, it was a bloody miracle that I forged any kind of livestock auction house in Lower Albany - an African miracle.

Keeping the buyers coming back was an art form - entice, give a little, take a little, play one off against another by creating a fear of loss. It was known full well that there were plots against the house at every turn. Livestock buyers are some of the sharpest minds I have ever encountered - 'no flies' on these boys! Occasionally I would meet old school gentlemen, long in the game. The Officer was the epitome of old time manners and a sabre sharp mind. In a fast paced, multiple bidding situation each buyer communicated with unique buying signals. It is possible that the auctioneer will drop the bid (trust me, it happens in the best of families)! The Officer always assumed the moral high ground and protected the bid, ready to 'stand on' saving my backside and offering protection.

The classing, sorting and presenting stock properly is a very important part to achieving true financial indicators in the ring. If the stock is not parcelled correctly ... you lose money - bottom line. 'The Cricketer' was a valuable and trusted member of my Manley Flats team. He knew cattle and could parcel livestock beautifully. The opposition were always looking for a 'floor crossing' and eventually they got it right. This turn of events sucker punched me, it was never the same after his departure. This turn of events prompted a change from livestock sales to catalogue game sales and I bid Manley Flats farewell.

04

AN INTRODUCTION TO PLAKKIES

A livestock auction yard attracts colourful characters - opportunists, gamblers, high rollers and desperados! I can guarantee you that at any given time, at any given auction, all of the above mentioned character types will be prevalent. At one stage, the high rollers would have been desperados and vice versa. In essence every character type is a gambler. In the livestock world, 'the house' never loses ...

When 'Plakkies' sauntered into my Hill Street office he presented a facade of high roller confidence, yet the edgy desperado status hung about him like fruit on a sausage tree. I never saw this man wear closed shoes, ever - standard issue was plakkies, PT shorts and a T-shirt. His blue eyes had a shield that locked out any attempt of soul searching and comfortably camouflaged his true arachnid capabilities.

The 'last outpost' is home to many of Zulu origin and, along with that heritage, comes an indelible link to ancestor worship and and a vibrant connection of the people to livestock and the use of ritual slaughtering. This in an effort to appease the aunt, uncle, sister, brother, mother, and father that have taken up their positions in the spirit world.

Goats and cattle are an important part of the worship cycle and this component of the livestock industry creates space for traders and speculators like Plakkies.

Now, very few traders are cash positive. Auction terms are seven days from sale. These terms do assist traders and speculators but we all know 'time flies when you're having fun'. In the case of Plakkies, three days were consumed by the transport of livestock purchased, then standing over a period of another two days to two weeks before the profit or loss reveals itself. The trading life is one fraught with cash flow issues and risk taking - animals die, road accidents are real and theft is a national sport in this arena.

Plakkies was needing stock and cash flow - of which I had both. I duly invited him to the first Nguni type cattle sale at Manley Flats and unleashed his newfound buying power on the likes of 'Krokodil' and he came up trumps, chasing prices up on every lot. On this day, Plakkies saved my bacon and rescued me from falling into a financial abyss - all the calves from Queenstown fetched top dollar and I winked at Fudu as lot after lot skyrocketed in price. After the sale, Fudu joined me in the bar (not to partake in liquor, he is teetotal). This gentleman prefers 'mountain cabbage'. Fudu is rather anti-establishment and stood there taking in the moment with the 'new kid on the block'.

05

PLAKKIES CONTINUED

"Engelsman waar's jou geld?" Gawie Grootbaard was in no mood for pleasantries or enquiring after my disposition. As the 'penny dropped' and I realised that the Seven Fountains auction revenue had not been paid to GBG, the mobile handset cradled to my ear became rather slick in my palm, rivulets of moisture pooled up in the fleshy architecture of my epidermis. Again the enquiry regarding funds, this time Mr Grootbaard's controlled and lingering pauses between words indicated his absolute need for clarity and understanding. At this point I will transport you to the Seven Fountains stock sale in question and the subsequent goat deal with Plakkies on the following morning.

Every auctioneer worth his salt always has a game plan! Some plans I witnessed were just downright dastardly, but, for the most part, an auctioneer has to pander, coerce and cajole. In short, an auctioneer will make you feel like a king or simply bully you into submission. There is always the promise of a better tomorrow - hope and the promise of financial gain keeps the human spirit alive and the promise of financial gain; and keeps the fear of loss at bay (keep the carrot dangling). However, beware the 'buyer's ring'. As an auctioneer you have to be able to divide and rule; if a group of buyers collude to regulate the floor price, you have a major problem. Seven Fountains Showtime - Obelix is rigging up my sound and I am taking note of buyers seated in the tent. A couple of big guns are present - Grensvegter from Perseverance, 'Maverick' from Thorn hill, The Officer, a handful of farmers and on the outside, 'Twitch' from Martindale and ... Plakkies. Today's offering comprises mostly oxen and small stock. Obelix and I are ready to spot, signal and call the closing bids while I wield my prized gavel.

The opening lot is ushered into the sales pen - a large, yellow haired ox, tall at the shoulder with expansive, raked back horns. It is a fairly decent offering to get the juices flowing. I double tap the gavel, signalling the floor is live and I open the bidding at ten thousand rand ... No reaction ... nine thousand rand, eight thousand rand; surely at six thousand rand? Grensvegter bites into his burger and signals intent with a cocked eyebrow and a low forward motion of his head, an almost unnoticeable gesture. Something is up! The usual legionnaires have left the field and after a few short strikes, Grensvegter steals the ox for seven thousand five hundred rand. Obelix my trusted spotter and scribe, whispers a sideways warning! "Hutch, we are in shit here! Buyers' ring of note!" The next few lots are soft to say the least and I sense growing concern amongst the sellers. "Obelix, stop the oxen, change the line up and bring in the weaners." I whisper, while cupping my hand over the headset microphone. Lightweight bull calves start entering the ring, looking furtively at the encamped splodge of humanity. One of the calves jumps nervously and sets the rest off in an explosion of hooves, swishing tails and a bawling noise. I take my cue and charge the lot with a mid-weight bid per kilogram. The change in energy electrifies the buyers and it's every man for himself! Plakkies turns his attention away from the pretty lady farmer and joins the foray. Bids are fierce and Plakkies openly displays his intent and outbids the big guns to take the lot. The buyers' ring has turned itself 'inside out' and the collusion tactics have backfired, destroying trust and ruining a few relationships while digging up 'old bones' of discontent amongst the buyers themselves. Order is restored and Plakkies leads the pack, edging out all comers. Lot after lot! The obvious intent of Plakkies' ambition sets the alarm bells ringing - this chap is trying to buy the whole auction. Non-payment in the auctioneering world of livestock is a fairly common occurrence. After having been 'shafted' on more than one occasion, my gut instinct geared me towards joining forces with a bigger, financially stronger auction house - all hail GBG lewendehawe! Oom Gawie and I struck a deal which allowed GBG a foothold in Lower Albany boosting the divisions T/O. Their footprint expanded into Settler territory and they could challenge 'the other guys' directly. My days as a financial risk taker were over and I slept easier at night. On this day, came the final tap of the gavel, the last chant and the clearing out of the sales pens, Plakkies was king. I remember looking out over the remnants of the buyers and sellers with Plakkies holding court, as if to the manor borne.

Insatiable is the only term to describe Plakkies desire for livestock. The KZN trade season was in full swing. Livestock sales are a numbers game; at three and a half per cent commission from the parent company, I had to capitalise on this opportunity. The next day I met with Plakkies and took him to view a few hundred Angora goats in Somerset East. The Karoo is a special place and the old stone kraals always fascinated me. Many, if not all of the stone walls and kraals dotted about on stock farms in the Eastern Cape were built by starving amaXhosa who flooded across the Fish River in search of sustenance after the great cattle killing which decimated the amaXhosa herds. The slaughtering of the amaXhosa cattle herds was urged on by a prophetess - Nongqawuse - various schools of thought and narrative abound surrounding this catastrophic event in the history of the amaXhosa people. Approximately 400 thousand livestock were destroyed and 40 thousand amaXhosa starved to death during the years 1856 - 1857.

Plakkies and I worked in the timeless, magnetic capsule of African spirituality - the kraal. While the Angoras scattered and regrouped into their social pods, we moved through them. Plakkies grabbed one here and there, inspecting teeth, horns and the general health of the animals. Once Plakkies had satisfied himself as to the quality and pertinence of the stock to his market, I observed his change in stance and body language. He wanted the animals and, through grinding molars and a clenched jaw, he started chipping away at the asking price. He toked on the cancer stick he held deftly between index finger and thumb. Lips lightly encompassing the filter end, he sucked on the wrapped tobacco, making the cigarette end glow brightly in the early morning light of the Karoo dawn. Plakkies had only one agenda, buy the animals and 'moer' the agent thus diminishing the agent's cut! Turning the agent's commission into a stumbling block is an old buyer's tactic. "So Hutch, is this a Frontier farming deal ... Or a GBG deal?" Plakkies had played his joker card. For the first time in all my dealings with Plakkies, I could penetrate his hooded gaze, allowing me a glimpse of the 'spider-like' weave of his conscious makeup. My stomach lurched. "It's a GBG sale", I said quietly. I sensed that Plakkies and I had reached the end of the road and that I may have dodged a bullet on that early Karoo morning. This was confirmed by the present phone call. Plakkies never did pay for the Seven Fountains stock nor the Angora goats in full. I would have been assassinated financially by Plakkies had this auction and stock deal not been under the auspices of GBG. Dankie Oom Gawie.

06

QUEENSTOWN CATASTROPHE

I watched intently, noticing the dark, yellowy-brown stains embedded into the thumbs and forefingers of the man deftly rolling a fat zol in his farmhouse kitchen. In the background his lovely wife busied herself, rustling up a splendid farm-style breakfast. It was 05:30 on a Thursday morning.

Fudu looked up at me for a long drawn out sigh and simply stated - "Hutch, they going to eat you for breakfast." I replied, "I know," - that was a long slow response. While I sat there and contemplated my most uncertain future, I was beyond grateful for Fudu's help until this point. The marijuana smoke hung heavy in the kitchen and Fudu nodded sagely while he took a deep draw down on the fatness of his holy leaf. He never consumed alcohol.

The triple deck interlink, loaded with one hundred twenty Nguni cross heifers and tolllies had been delayed in its departure from Queenstown, the day before. The stock was headed to Manley Flats, where I hosted numerous Nguni type cattle sales. Today's auction was billed as the biggest ever - Nguni type cattle sale! And right now, I was 'seeing my arse, without a mirror'.

Around eight the previous evening, the heavens had opened and rain had pelted down. Usually the sound of rain provided a comforting background sound to a restful night. Not on this occasion ... I tossed and turned, expecting the worst. No contact with the Queenstown truck brought a sense of foreboding. On answering my cell around midnight I heard: "Oom!" the exaggerated greeting pierced my eardrum - 'The cattle are dying on the truck!'

I picked up The Apprentice and we raced out into the dark and wet night. We found the truck just outside Fort Beaufort. In the wet, the calves had slipped and fallen about in large numbers on the upper and lower decks. The Apprentice sprang into action! He fought his way through the melee of flailing hooves, bawling calves and three inches of fresh, slippery cowshit. All the while, the rain came down. It was then that I noticed the underlying problem ... The driver had gone off the road and had sunk the behemoth up to the axles in soft mud. I looked around in the darkness and falling rain, shaking my head in an attempt to rid my vision of the blinding torrential downpour that engulfed us.

Safe to say, I had no language for the driver! I had to solve this logistical nightmare and quickly. The calves were The Apprentice's dept ... I had to get this truck moving and the calves offloaded at Manley flats ASAP. The biggest Nguni type cattle sale ever, was hours from the opening bell.

The dull, yellow light of a far off farmhouse managed to flicker its way to my retina, pulsing weakly through the sheet rain. The flickering light represented hope and I was in need of salvation. I knew not who I would find at this farmhouse. Imagine my surprise when local legend - Fudu opened the door and recognised me standing there in the wet darkness, dripping puddles onto his stoep at three a.m..

A brief exchange and Fudu swung back the doors of his tractor shed ... When I saw the big, yellow Caterpillar machine ... I couldn't believe it! We had a fighting chance to get this truck back on the road. Hallelujah!

Fudu pushed that machine to its limits, bucking and straining, digging in the bucket, scoring the tar surface, with steel teeth biting and gripping; while he inch wormed that truck back onto the tar. "Fudu, you beaut!" I shouted above the revving diesel engines. He just took a blow of 'Ganga' to his chest and gave a deep chuckle. "Hutch, come for breakfast."

We soaked up the moment and enjoyed the warmth of the farmhouse kitchen. Fudu had saved the day. Now, I had to prep The Cricketer so he could slot these calves into a decent sale plan. When I ascended the podium, Obelix was like ... "You have an odour, a sweet one at that ..." Fudu was at the ringside when the opening bids came rolling in. "Thank you Fudu." - Jah love.

07

ZUURBERG STORM

Myself and the Apprentice are in the back end of the Zuurberg, Addo area - I have been summoned by Emilio, the Spaniard, to come and assist with livestock he has on his property. On the way to the Spaniard, I'm thinking ... what does Emilio know about cattle ... and I wonder which of these Lower Albany operators have pulled a move on this chap? The thing about Emilio was that he only ever called when he found himself a little 'screwed over', which was fairly often.

I met Emilio when he was looking around for a farm to buy. I showed him a few Fish River farms and I remember him being keen on the one property, but he had also seen a property in Addo ... "Mr Haandrew, I also see theeeez one farm, nice in Addo, can I buy theeez farm wit you or dat one Mr Haaandrew?" I replied, "Emilio, please go and buy the farm in Addo, it's a better plan." That's how I got to know Emilio ...

On arrival at Emilio's spread, we headed straight to his makeshift cattle crush. II was horrified at the state of the cattle in the crush. My spoken words of dismay were hardly cold when The Apprentice shouted that there were cattle falling over in the crush. We started injecting the cattle one by one, starting from the rear of the long crush and worked our way forwards. For some it was too late, they expired right there at our feet. Their rolling orbits for eyes accompanied the desperate flailing hooves gouging the wet earth. Both heart water and Asiatic redwater took their toll while the heavens opened and water jettisoned from the sky - it was as if a New York firefighter had a fire hose trained on us. We worked the cattle 'til we ran out of needles and muti. The Apprentice and I were kicked, trodden and stamped on as we tried our best to save the lives of over a hundred head of cattle. Those that we could place on their hooves and steady were pushed through into the holding kraal. Sopping wet, aching in all departments and covered in bovine waste, we accepted the invitation to accompany Emilio up to the homestead.

Once I had cleaned up and changed into some clothing - donated by our host (which I still have to this day). I engaged with Emilio regarding the plethora of cattle on his property, their condition and their origin!

"Mr Haaandrew, theeza cow they are not for me! ... " Well, in the end I discovered Emilio was on a weight gain/profit split scheme with our man Plakkies. Now Plakkies was never going to be able to show Emilio a weight gain nor any kind of profit because the cattle were all dairy cross types and mostly stunted oxen, destined for the Zulu trade market. The sourveld conditions on the backside of the Zuurberg, combined with very little supplements to assist these beasts, and the fact that Plakkies could never leave them there through a growing season or attend to their needs, meant only one winner would emerge from this endeavour ... net effect equals cheap holding camps for Plakkies ... Poor Emilio had been railroaded ...

08

"FAWLTY TOWERS"

The baboon troop was truly at home. Some lay sprawled sideways, while a fellow trooper attended to the other's parasitic problems. A few just sat on their haunches, dozing in the sun. Their substantial rear ends were being warmed on the hot tin roof - the rusted tin roof of 'Fawlty Towers'.

Upon entering the foyer of this property, the decay was clearly evident. Frayed fabrics, musty odours and dark passages led to scary box-like chambers, devoid of windows or ventilation. Neglect wore a dark cloak as it loitered about the spaces of this once lively roadside hotel and watering hole. I pushed open the hollow, panelled, brown door to the deserted bar area. Hinges retching in protest, the perforated, damaged portal tracked ninety degrees intermittently, allowed me passage to cross the threshold into this mortuary of past revelry. The old, illuminated Black Label beer fridge whirred and hummed inconsistently. The near empty racks were barely visible through the settled grime and mature mould spores. Every few seconds the flywheel on the archaic motor stretched the worn-out belt causing the power to stumble and slip, fracturing the illumination from the battered Black Label sign as it winked and blinked like a dying star in a black hole of nothing.

My pupils dilated trying to gather form and depth in the gathered dusk of this fetid space.

The nicotine sponged itself off the faded wallpaper and a single upward curl of smoke lazily suggested a hint of life in this dark junction of middle earth. It loosely gathered itself up from the orange, hexagonal ashtray. I made out the large shadow of a slouched male person, lying as a dead weight half on the bar counter ... All the while, the baboon troop played out their antics overhead.

I half bent over, closing in for a better visual of this person trying his level best to impersonate a departed soul. The left eyelid had a R.E.M. moment, giving away a clue to vague consciousness. The waft of hard liquor, days of unwashed body odour and a multitude of stubbed out cigarette butts were festooned about on the short, square panels of worn out carpet. The right side of the man's head and cheek was squished, flattened out onto the drinks' drip tray. The circular cut-outs on the brass cover created pinched bubble wrap prints on the fleshy, loose, biomass of his cheek. I saw this facial sculpture, as he lifted his head, turning to face me. His eyes looked like shrivelled up guavas, looking for relief after years of drought, connected to a stunted desert of a mother tree.

I located a light switch and a yellow atmosphere cocooned the wasted brain of 'Basil' - I had found the owner of this defunct hostelry.

Cigarette ash and hardened dandruff matted together, forming a false scalp under the course orangey-brown head of 'kroes' cushioning attached to his throbbing skull. I felt Basil's pain as he gesticulated wildly with a loose, flapping left arm. Hoarse, he mouthed the words - "Sell dis farkin place!" - before collapsing back onto the bar top, right hand now conducting a blind search for any vestibule of liquid that maybe sat on the old oak bar counter. His octopus arm knocked over a highball glass, it fell into the service area between the bar and fridge. I heard not the expecting shattering of glass but rather a soft 'glump' - odd, I thought and peered over the counter top. Spread eagled on the melamine floor of honeycomb pattern, lay a young chap. Short, military style brush cut, half clad in camo pants, he lay 'kaal bolyf' on his back, the fallen glass magnifying his belly button. A deep gash distorted his right eyebrow and his eye socket bore a purple-tinge of colour. He was staring up at the pressed ceiling. Only when he blinked, did I banish my internal screams of "Corpse!"

The youngster on the floor seemed ambivalent to my presence. I suggested he should try and sit up. He did better than that, he pushed up off the melamine and stood, supporting his body weight with downward bent palms on the ice machine of sorts. The split, raised eyebrow caused his eye to look like a tree frog, backed up into a weathered knot in the bark of a blue gum tree. As he weaved, unsteady on his feet, he spoke - "Sorry, Oom, we are pissed." To wrap up, Basil wheezed, "Where's the papers? Sell the farkin place!" I manoeuvred around to Basil's limited field of cognisance. "When I come back here in two days' time from now (gesturing with two fingers), you better be sober, and this youngster should be dressed." I slowly mouthed the words at a decent decibel of sound. Basil's guava-like eyes blinked and he lifted a hand in a slow measurement of compliant understanding, and all the while the baboons righted the wrongs of their world on the roof.

Two days later, I returned to Fawlty Towers and this time, Basil was able to converse, but not much more than that. There was no way he could sign any mandate instructions. On my third visit, he was of sober mind, hands shaking, in need of a drink but thankfully sober. I took him through the auction mandate and he put a scrawled, squiggled, cosmos of a signature on the mandate document. No sooner were the signature and initials committed to each page, when he summoned the 'Cammo Kid': "Gooi whiskey," he half pleaded with the youngster. I took that as my cue and left to begin the marketing for his auction date.

The objections came thick 'n fast. "That's a lot of sqm under rusted baboon piss." - "Does it even have water?" - "What about the outstanding rates amount?" And the topper - "Basil will never leave!" - and many more objections sprouted from canvassed buyers.

I continued to advertise and canvass my database of contacts. A few prospectus manuals were requested, but there was no groundswell of interest. The auction date arrived and Obelix and I set up our bidding hall in the reception area. I have impressed it upon Basil - do not interfere with proceedings, do not interact with potential bidders - stay away!

'Basil' and 'the Cammo Kid' hole up in the receptionist's office. The two of them resemble the primates that are cavorting along the rusted roof capping. They observe the goings on with craned necks, furtive glances and hooded brows.

Some folk arrive and leave, a few mill around outside, causing the troop some consternation. They sense something is up!

Obelix rings the first bell and calls intrepid 'snoopers' out from the dark passageways and hidey-holes. The second bell finds five seated parties, each with a bidder's card and terms and conditions of sale. It's a bleak picture ... Of the five, I might sequester bids from two ... maybe three?

There's no point to pissing around here. I start the bid at a God awful low number. All of the mercenaries 'gimme the greenlight'.

They've come to grab what they can today. Raising the bid by increments of ten thousand rand, I try to stretch the race to the finish line, encouraging testosterone belligerence, seeking out the Alpha! The Alpha is not always the brash, confident peacock in the room; most times it's the quiet, mindful, focused individual.

We passed the one million rand mark and it's down to two - 'Garfield' and 'Bin Laden'. Both bidders have an equal chance of being the other's nemesis today. A property auction is vastly different to that of livestock or loose goods; the bid call is slower ... lingering ... and confirmation of the bid lends focus on the potential buyer, reminding other bidders that they have opposition. Obelix occupies himself with captivating Bin Laden and I walk the floor, firm and concise in my engagement with Garfield. I up the ante with a flourish of a hundred thousand rand increments - no opposition. I take Obelix's point at two million rand - Garfield falters at two million one hundred thousand rand ... "The bid stands firm at two million rand, are you in at two million one hundred thousand rand, Sir?" A slow shake of the head, negative! Garfield is out. The bid falls back on Bin Laden and I confirm the top bid of R2m. I know it's way short but it's an offer! As I confirm the top bid of two million rand and clarify that I will revert, subject to confirmation, the door to the receptionist's office bursts open! It overrides its hinges and thwacks into the inside wood panelling.

Basil staggers out with Cammo Kid barrelling along behind him. "Fark off you, Grahamstown people, fark off with your money." Basil's vocal chords are doing the Highland fling as he curses us all. I see the whites of Obelix's eyes and the OMG round-mouthed look of surprise. Basil kicks chairs over and exits the auction area, heading for oblivion, down the dark passageway. The Cammo Kid covers their retreat, middle finger on parade! Not quite sure of his target, he acquires a blanket approach and extends the invitation to all too ... "Sit and swivel."

Outside, in the car park, Bin Laden comes up to me. Behind his spectacles, inquisitive lines pinch his eyelids and round up his cheeks. "How much does he want?" Referring to Basil, he displays intent with a mischievous charm. Stroking his abundant and long facial hair, Bin Laden is looking for a deal. I don't pull any punches and make the figure known - "Four million five hundred thousand million rand!" Bin Laden doesn't skip a beat, "OK," he says ... "OK, what!?" I say - "OK, I buy for four million five hundred thousand million rand!" He says. The completed word structure of WTF comes out of my mouth and I ask, "Why did you stop bidding?" Bin Laden casts a look at me, half confused. "Boss, your prospectus said - cash on the day. I only have two million rand in cash, under here." He points to his flowing robe ...

The baboons - disturbed by all the activity - 'fireman slide' down the askew drainage pipes. The troop hit the ground, running amuck amongst a new bunch of 'tyre kickers'. The teardrop banners have lured more people off the N2 highway for a gander. There's not much I can do about the baboons, but I can do something about this offer!

Basil has the whisky bottle in a death grip, lips tight to the bottle neck. Adam's apple chugs up and down as the malt whiskey flash floods down his throat. I'm too late, ten min too late. His eyes roll back in his head, its tickets and there is no sense to be had from Cammo Kid.

Three weeks pass. My phone rings ... Unknown number. I answer to Basil's voice, "Where's ve money?" "Excuse me?" I'm flabbergasted in my response. "Bring ve money!" Basil insists. I finish this crazy call and beeline it for Bin Laden's office. Bin Laden sits across his desk from me. "That money is finish now, how can I buy now?" The bright eyes shift their focus and he stares at the ceiling for what seems like an age. "Go tell that man one million six hundred thousand rand, that's all!" I contemplate his plea of poverty and this latest instruction ...

Basil is as sober as a judge upon my arrival. I put him and Cammo Kid into the bakkie and headed for a conveyancer's office. We have to wait awhile; 'Peggy Sue' is busy. Bin Laden is on his way. Basil has started with the shakes and Cammo Kid is already 'tuning' him as to what they going to do with the MOOLAH! Basil just wants a drink, I can see the sense of reasonability starting to disappear, 'Like mist before the morning sun'. "Hurry up!" I mentalise with Peggy Sue.

Bin Laden arrives and we consult with Peggy Sue – she dictates the sales document and we conclude matters! - 'pheeew'.

Basil loses a fortune but we achieve some 'get out of jail' money for him, and the property is sold - voetstoots! - No comebacks, as is.

Not long after this. I am back in Peggy Sue's office with Basil and Bin Laden. It's a bit crowded and Cammo Kid waits outside the door … a look of anticipation on his face. We close the door and at that Basil goes mental! He is claiming the deposit, threatening to cancel the sale etc. Now, Bin Laden is a shrewd operator, he calmly surveys the scene and asks Basil, "You want money?" Basil's fingers are drumming out an anxious beat on the bent, wooden arms of the high back chair he occupies. Bin laden doesn't wait for an answer from the jaundiced Basil. He writes out a cash cheque for twenty thousand rand - holding the promise of payment up for all to see. Basil snatches the rectangle of relief from Bin Laden's fingers and heads for the door. Cammo Kid is at the ready, looking like a relay runner on the home straight. Basil hands the cheque to him and he bounds down the stairs like a mountain goat. Bin Laden knocks another fifty thousand rand off the agreed selling price - Basil submits and we are all poorer for it.

Cammo Kid cashes the cheque, assumes the role of 'pied piper' and leads Basil to liquor langsyne. I am left wondering ... Will Basil even survive until the date of registration of transfer? Will his liver hold out? It's all on 'a lick and a promise' at this point.

The property is finally registered in Bin Laden's nominated structure and Basil vacates. At the last count, the baboons had moved out and renovations were in full swing, preparing the property for another period of a different sort of subterfuge ...

09

BIG BIRD DEALINGS

Let's face it! Property auctions are where the real money can be found. Fixed property does sell, to the right buyer eventually. Conventional property agents market multitudes of fixed property or real estate around the globe, on a daily basis. In comparison, auctions have the ability to achieve an expedient result for a seller. Interest in the given property is stimulated through accentuated attention from buyers, attracted by the idea of a competitive price option. The seller incurs advertising costs and the buyer pays commission. This modus operandi can represent a significant saving for the vendor. 'On auction' sales material attracts a significant number of bargain hunters, which in turn stimulates and creates interest and dialogue between all parties - auctioneer, buyers, seller and speculators. The auction process sifts the straw from the wheat and the men from the boys. 'Tyre kickers' are swiftly identified and a base of qualified parties is established with some alacrity.

Fixed property sales come with emotion, history, relationship issues, deceased estates and financial distress. In many cases, a sale of property brings much needed relief to the seller. A commercial property may be the centre of a hostile takeover or the dissolution or liquidation of a business or partnership. In some aspects, 'mafia' movies and market domination can force the sale and closure of a commercial or production facility. In such a case, there are many internal issues and political wrangling to deal with! Whichever way the property is

41

mandated to an auctioneer - closed tender bids or public auction, this is a lucrative instruction for the auctioneer of choice.

However, the puff adder in the panicum - a source of danger to the instructed auctioneer - can be that there is no clear intent to dispose of the property in question.

Or that the company is seeking to release the premises on condition that historical activities must cease. On top of this, the seller may be preparing their preferred buyer on the sideline, unbeknown to the auctioneer. In due course, the auctioneer becomes an unwitting chess piece in this game of 'Giants'.

I was instructed to sell by public auction, a building and business premises afflicted by most of the above issues.

My initial enthusiasm knew no bounds and I canvassed long and hard. It was a very specific property, used for a very specific purpose. I saw past those 'pigeonhole' restrictions and concentrated on marketing the location, multiple title deeds, and multiple usage possibilities - there was a noxious trade zoning in place, opening up all kinds of trade possibilities from the premises. Furthermore, the property and improvements were to be sold - 'Lock, stock and barrel'. A large amount of loose goods and equipment were attached to the property inventory.

The property appealed to a number of investors on my database. I was cautiously optimistic as to a positive outcome!

Displacement of my enthusiasm arose, when previously employed staff members began querying whether they would receive salary payments still owed by the holding company, on the day of the auction …? Amber light flashing for Hutchinson.

Showing the property and facilities was a rather creepy affair. The electricity was disconnected … Moving about from hall to hall and to the massive cold storage areas was a little unsettling in the dark. In the processing areas, chains and hooks hung ominously and sometimes these villainous bits of hardware held a slight sway, a miniscule movement, where there should be none. Torch batteries expired mid-viewing and if you were night blind, there wasn't much to take in.

Anyway, I was to sell, by public auction, this behemoth of a building to the highest bidder that exceeded the reserve price.

The turnout on the day was fairly impressive - all of my shortlisted buyers arrived! These were then backed up by a fair few 'Tyre kickers' and happy hopefuls! A Western Cape vehicle unloads a five party secondment … "Interesting," I thought. These chaps take up a position near the front of the concentric, curved layer of seating. 'Show goers' are filing in; Obelix records all attending individuals and processes the buyers' cards as required. There is a mixed level of charge in the air … Angst, expectation and latent greed, patch a band aid over the uncertainties of some of the auction attendees.

I take the time, as usual, to assess the floor and the 'show goers'. Four of my interested parties have taken up positions to the rear of the seating arrangement.

"This is going to be good," I whisper to Obelix. In my mind's eye, I start playing out the possible block changing algorithm of this auction. I'm preparing for opening bids from this quarter, midrange 'adventure' bids from that quarter and from where I expect the final tussle to emanate. Garfield is a strong contender today! I aim to govern his entry into the game until late in the exchange, fresh legs to carry me in the home straight and push the mid-range pundits.

Hunting for the bid should be a 'honeypot' affair; this property has attracted the prosperous pockets!

Krokodil is on the far left, a strong outside contender; he represents a massively strong outfit.

The Western Cape contingent is chatting in hushed tones amongst themselves. There appears to be a disagreement of sorts brewing in their camp. Scowls, set jaws, fingers strumming hectic riffs on their cross armed postures. Leaning in towards each other on the exchange ... this is not a united front! It's plain as day, this crew has an agenda!

It's time! Terms and conditions are read out, property and title deed information confirmed and a little window dressing for good measure. There are some big guns here today ... Obelix has a slight sheen on his forehead ... Not just from the warmth of the day ... he's excited.

My opening bid call is drawn out and solid ... my outstretched arm looking for the strong soldier. Heads swivel in the direction of my ranged plea. Krokodil takes a drag on his smoke and rolls his eyes to the sky. Deadpan, disinterested, poker face - Krokodil is well known to the community present and everyone is aware of the financial punch he packs. Dropping steadily through the financial quarters, still confident of a mid-range strike ... there comes nothing. In the coming seconds, I challenge the initial Rubick's Cube block chain I had planned out! Swopping my body stance, I reach out to the far right corner - Garfield must come in now! The time is right and he's got legs. Surely! He must come in? A low cast shake of the head, negative! I'm stupefied. My bid call continues, unrepentant and everclear ... The floor looks like a big fish tank ... And my voice sounds muffled, as if underwater. This can't be happening?

Still no takers! Obelix and I are both sweating now. My eyes are raking the crowd; I don't see the catalyst I'm looking for. It's a negative space. There's only one option, I cut to the chase, bottoming out at an absolute bargain basement figure ... Interestingly, as I run through the numbers, heading to negative territory, the Western Cape contingent sit fairly relaxed and nonchalant. Their initial angst seems to have dissipated. I still can't figure this gang out.

I'm rock-bottom and my voice is a little strained, looking for the safety net ... *BAM*! Garfield picks up the bid, its game on! Easing the players into the game, I pitch ten thousand rand increments. The Western Cape outfit, Krokodil and a couple of aspirant chargers all go for the honey! It's an easy bid, well below any kind of market value. I'm using the idea of a cheap bid to build the momentum. The early bidders are enjoying the engagement ... We all know how this ends for them, but I'm grateful for their 'fire lighting' favour!

Following the favour, I allow them to savour the moment and the idea that they own the day.

The rattle and hum and staccato bids increase in tempo. My vocals, pitching and softening, pitching again, calling in the worker bees and focusing on the honey!

Body posture full of confidence, brought on by the swarm of bids, I edge out the bottom feeders and bring the main players into the gambit.

Suddenly we have an auction! This Rubick's Cube is changing slots quicker than the commodities schedule on the Johannesburg stock exchange! This auction is in danger of over running itself - time to manage the bid, by time and engagement with each bidder.

Slow the game down, keep everyone in the hunt! The assisted pressure on the bidders keeps the numbers running and we pass the mandated figure! The Western Cape wranglers sink low into their seats! Disbelief and consternation cloud their collective demeanours. Still, the bid runs. The pitch and tone value of my voice ratchet in the chain of bids. The race is on; we've come through the storm! It's time to claim the pot of gold at the end of the rainbow. Garfield finds the final knock of the gavel. He looks like the proverbial cat that got the cream! I complete proceedings with a flourish of thank yous and the statutory - subject to confirmation parting shot; I wrap up the business at hand.

I am outside planning the tiger fishing trip of a lifetime with Obelix when I hear a call for all shareholders to convene in the boardroom ... "This does not bode well," I say to Obelix. I'm feeling uneasy, with a furrowed brow. Sometime later, the shareholders emerge and the elected spokesman apologises to one and all ... Essaying an explanation to the tune of incomplete financials and simply stating, the property may not be sold, as a result of this situation.

Well, blow me down with a feather! WTF? To cut a long story

short, the bid was not accepted as a binding sale and I was left high and dry. A few months later I was re-instructed to dispose of the property via means of a closed bid tender. This time, the bid was accepted and the eventual buyers were ... "The Western Cape wranglers." Industry mafia and market forces claimed number one spot on the podium. The property was mothballed and stood vacant for months thereafter. I later resold it with the assistance of another industry connection. That's a story for another day!

10

PIG STORIES

A pig has a definitive eye! Second only to a goat, a pig's eye will impart the mood or the intent of the creature.

A pig has its own differential and leaves little for the mind's eye. The 'piggy eye' is like the dark side of the moon - inhospitable and unwelcoming!

On a hot summers' day I travelled up to Adelaide. I was due to show a farm property to 'Smurf & Smurfette'. Travelling out on the Waterkloof Road from town, I notice how dry the area is. "Jeez, it's dry." I wonder how the Kudus and warthogs are faring. Dams are empty and the red clay earth is openly exposed between the stands of Spekboom and thorn trees. Stock fences are a hindrance to Kudus and the like, during extended periods of drought. The weakened antelope don't have the strength to clear the barrier and usually get their hind legs caught up in the top two strands - a hapless situation for the strength-sapped animal.

Little did I know the impact a boundary - netting wire fence - would have on me later in the day!

I duly arrived at the farm gate. Before I can open the padlock, I notice a beat up old Ford Bantam bakkie, driving slowly towards my position. A loose arrangement of 'bushwhackers' are perched on the back of the vehicle and to the left of the slow moving vehicle, I notice a few affiliates from the Bantam bakkie

- whistling and beating the netting wire fence with sticks. "What the hell are these whackers up to now?" I think to myself.

The veld on the inside of the netting wire fence is scrubbed short. Stubbed, brown-ended, curled nibs of forgotten nourishment are sparse. The remnants of past sweetness spider crawl to nowhere in particular, atop the parched, dry earth.

In contrast, the verge between the road and the fence has knee high Digitaria growing thick! This pantry of fodder conceals the approaching danger ... The Bantam bakkie slows to regain the fence 'operatives' and then speeds past me. The rear springs of the vehicle are splayed flat with the combined weight of all the occupants. The front wheels are barely in touch with the road surface. Corrugations on the poorly maintained road create an unstable, multiple bounce for the depressed tyres, kicking up an inordinate amount of dust!

Minute particles of red earth congeal about my eyelids, ears and nostrils. It is a wind free day and the disturbed freckles of dust hang in the air like a fine coating of talcum powder. Visibility is limited ... but I can hear the netting wire fence is being tested by a body of volume that is bashing into the barrier repeatedly. The probing attack on the fence line is frenzied and ferocious! Clearly, the 'bushwhackers' have herded a creature of sorts towards me along the fence line. The atmosphere is thick and the fence basher has gone quiet. I cock an ear and shield my brow with an outstretched hand. I peer, blurrily, at the last point of sound. The thick curtain of Digitaria is parted and an impressive oxbow of ivory presents itself. A flat, shovel of a face and double wart-like protrusions come into view! It's a bloody pig!

The warthog boar launches an attack from the long grass. 'Pumba' barrels into me, teeth switchblade for a strike on my legs! I see long cadavers of polished ivory trying to puncture me. I couldn't believe it - a bastard of a thing, gnashing and striking at me with true intent. The hog looks up at me, seeking eye contact! The absolute animalism of this 'piggy eye' washes the red freckles of earth aside, as I blink and focus on my attacker. The swine is twisting, hooking and biting with its fearsome dentistry. If this pig strikes an artery, I'm goners!

The forward incisors are needle sharp points with an inside, sharp edge, running down into the basement of the animal's maw. The aerial display from this fat, muscle wrapped thug, resplendent in its red dust tunic is incredible - jumping, bucking and pirouetting while employing its fearsome dentistry in its aim to damage me. The imminent danger converts everything into slow motion ... The devastating ugliness of this beast consumes my visual aspect: besides the devilish attack by the business end of the pig, I notice the parted lips, populated with coarse bunions of single hair follicles planted between other bumps and lumps. It's a nightmare of a creation ... No wonder it's pissed off!

My Maasai approach to escaping the gnashing porker - up and down like a pogo - doesn't work. The attacker simply waits until gravity negates my upward leap and then intensifies the biting, hooking and lunging effort. My brain is screaming - self-preservation!

A Scottish approach to the psycho swine manifests itself in a Highland fling type of dance! My knees are up to my chest, arms flailing about in quick succession. All this is happening as Smurf and Smurfette arrive. Windows up, they escape the 'bushwhackers' dust. I can see the two of them, laughing their heads off! No one comes to my assistance.

The hog's nerve finally breaks and he pivots in the air, breaking ground with all four trotters upon landing. Galloping away at full speed, he collides with the wire on the farm gate - Twang! The high tensile, steel wire snaps like a piano wire under duress.

The two in the newly arrived vehicle, are beside themselves with laughter! I am not on the same page. The 'bushwhackers' are parked a short way up the road, I hear the mutterings of discontent, as the pig bullets its way up the hill and out of sight.

Tucking my shirt in, I regain my composure and escort my clients around the property. They insist on driving behind me in their own truck ... Odd! Anyway, on we go and throughout the farm viewing, Smurfette declined all invitations to alight from the vehicle ... Months later, we meet up at a braai. As we chat, the pig incident comes up in the conversation. Smurfette admits to laughing so hard, that her bladder extended and she urinated, rendering her jeans sopping. The front seat of the vehicle resembled a pothole puddle in High Street, Grahamstown.

I never managed to sell that property by closed tender bids nor standard offer to purchase means - "The curse of the pig!"

Pigs are difficult animals to work with. That piggy eye has just got too much going on, one cannot fathom these creatures.

A Martindale farmer is overheard, waxing lyrical about his weaners. The Intel reaches me and I make work of it. Directions to the farm are easy enough but the road forks left ... I have never been down the left fork in this road. I am keen on these weaners! Manley Flats sale is looming and I need stock.

Now, you get off the beaten track and then you just get ... 'do-people-really-live-down-here' types of roads! "These weaners better be a class act," I think to myself as I negotiate the unstable and inconsistent road surface. Far off, down in the valley, a lone farmhouse creeps into view. Gut instinct whispers "Turn around," but no, Hutchinson doesn't listen. Bad roads damage your vehicle, no doubt, but they also steal time from the traveller! After an eternity of listening to my vehicle bemoaning its particular fate, I arrive at the farmhouse.

The farmer is excited and enthusiastic! "Wow!" You came all this way to see my weaners?

"Oh my word ..." That's all I have to say when he reveals, six ... A sum total of six! - piglets. A far cry from the beautiful weaner calves I was expecting. The curse of the pig! - "Aaargh."

The Apprentice seeks to convince me ... "These piglets will make money! But we have to load them in Queenstown." We arrive in due course to load thirty-six, squirming, piggies ... (Like I want to be doing this ... not!) The little buggers are slippery and quick as a flash. It becomes thirsty work loading these critters ... Luckily, Aloe Grove guest farm and pub is just down the road.

Upon our arrival at Aloe Grove we find marquee tents erected and open fires dotted about. Half the Winterberg and Stormberg communities are in attendance. Hell's bells, it's a party!

We find Oom Stan at one of the fire pits. "My boy, what brings you up the mountain," he asks jovially.

The Apprentice volunteers ... "I'm loading pigs Oom." Oom Stan looks at me, "How many piglets do you want?" he asks me. Well, we offloaded the first thirty-six into a warm, straw-filled storeroom and the next morning, we loaded our transport to capacity with more piglets, courtesy of Oom Stan!

In between, we partook of the finest hospitality and had a fat, farm style jol at the mini 'oxbraai'.

The piglets were duly offloaded at Manley's and I opened the small stock section of the auction with these bundles of bacon.

Astronomical prices bounced between the buyers. The curse was broken and I never canvassed for swine again.

11

QUEENSTOWN NGUNI CLUB SALE

They say good fences make good neighbours. Bonnox, barbed wire, high strain, veldspan - you name it and a farmer's Co-op can advise on a multitude of fencing options. Fences demarcate property boundaries, camp systems, secure areas and they can contain 'disease'.

Breeding / animal husbandry forms a large part of livestock and game keeping projects. Financial gain is the aim of most farmers, or custodians of creatures on the hoof. Fences are the first point of genetic manipulation. These barriers assist with the placing of a bull with a certain set of heifers, ensuring protected camps for lambing or calving and the isolation of females for artificial insemination.

The hand of man has touched the animal world in an irreversible manner. There is no such thing as free range. Outer Mongolia represents the largest expanse of pastoral freedom on the planet, but it too runs out of geography. This rock called earth that spins and rotates through a fixed orbit of endless cosmos, is a planet of controlled manipulation.

So, humans demarcate the planet with physical boundaries for genetic control and production of animal products. On top of this, humans place social boundaries around themselves. These camps of social aggregates or common denominators are thought to bring humans of certain cognitive thought processes together. However, humans are governed by many chemical and emotive responses, which amplify individual reactions.

To each person, interpretation and idea exchange is a large component that influences human condition and situation. The mobilisation of information and ideas between humans ultimately filters through to the animal kingdom. Animal husbandry / farming ideas are born out of collaboration between scientific studies and breeding study groups. Farmers love to tie themselves to clubs, societies, and associations. As a result, the above social and industrial structures are emotionally charged cages for humanity.

Photos in studbook journals are beautifully presented in colour, manipulated by computer programmes, and edited ink allotments on the printing press. These glossy encyclopaedias portray breeders and their charges in the best possible light. These publications entice and focus attention on the measured statistics of the given breed or animal. These printed pages of perception stimulate interest in a breeder's animals and ultimately his/her name. People buy brands in retail stores, as they do on auctions!

The difference is ... a livestock brand is affected by a multitude of environmental and man-made factors. An animal's virility, intercalving period, overall physical condition and rumen content are all affected by relocation to another geographical area. In some cases, just relocating to a different camp on the same property may pose risks! Adaptation to a new geographical environment can be challenging for the relocated animal. Every single statistic that promoted a buyer's interest could be lost or rendered null and void, due to parasites, quality of water, feed and temperature changes.

Preparation of animals for auctions is a reality. Sellers will feed bulls and put females into special camps for weeks before an auction. The glossy studbook ads corroborate the physical appearance of the beast standing in the viewing pen. Bulls are moved to sale pens days before an auction and are fed at the auction facility. This practice combats travel stress and mitigates loss of condition. Remember ... The bull's current condition is a falsehood! Once he starts working, he loses condition and doesn't look a patch on the studbook gloss! Tick populations can have a devastating effect on your prize bull you just bought on a stud auction! "I know, it happened to me." Heart water is a virulent, tick borne sickness that can wreak havoc amongst cattle not adapted to tick environments.

Auctioneers will duly noted animals from heart water areas, but they won't draw your attention to animals that have been prepared for the sale. They will rather extol the virtues of the beautifully presented beasts. All in all, clubs, societies and associations do not prohibit an animal's preparation for a sale. That ethos lies with the seller and herein grows the discontent of members or certain groups. Not everyone believes in window dressing their stock! Greed and jealousy start to govern a club or such like group; divisions are created. Character assassinations happen and breeding brands come under fire from supposed allies or comrades in arms.

One may call this pure politics; I prefer to call this - a state of pride and prejudice! All the club members or association subscribers are proud of their stock but they hold prejudice close to their hearts. Judging and rubbishing each other sublimely ... and sometimes quite publicly ... while the cattle just stand, waiting ... unaware.

I can make out a 'dust devil' in the distance, round and round it goes, climbing higher into the great expansive ceiling of the blue Karoo sky. Approaching the 'devil' in the open plains, I notice the base is sedentary; it is not gobbling up a path across the dry landscape. It cannot travel because the 'devil', is in fact, a massive sand storm being kicked up inside a circular kraal. A large collective of Nguni type calves is circling the edge of the wooden slatted kraal, bringing about a stationary twister!

I hazard a guess that these calves haven't seen the inside of a handling facility before ... skittish is a loose term to describe these weaners. I climb through the slats and sit quietly in the middle of the ring-a-rosy pantomime playing itself out. I always preferred circular handling facilities compared to square or rectangular kraals. The ferris wheel of calves eventually slows to a walk and a halt. As the next time travel capsule dissolves ... natural curiosity takes hold. Beautiful Nguni stories unfold around me - each calf is an acclaimed director of the drama unfolding on its hide. A splash of storytelling, which makes for full colour fun. The dark, wet noses and pretty, concise clear ears, point forward, pricked up - captured by curiosity. All of these calves are exclusive and distinctive, yet phenotypical of each other. I do not hesitate and purchase the lot of them. No strings attached. Over the next few days I canvas the surrounding area and secure a large amount of Nguni type cattle - destined for the Queenstown - East Cape Nguni club sale.

Leaving your sphere of influence and marketing an auction in a relatively unknown or socially disconnected area is a risk! In this particular case, I was two hundred twenty kilometres away from my support base, tending to a club that for all intents and purposes was just about defunct, with little or no stock from club members on the sale. Queenstown is full of 'red' cattle. The odds were against me. I had to make a plan!

"I made that plan!" I personally canvassed and trucked in more stock to that sale than the actual club members! Studbook sellers still had no idea that they were going to owe their existence to the unregistered segment of the Nguni livestock industry. The studbook sellers decried the arrival of the commercial animals. I had allies in the form of the 'buffalo soldier' and the 'brothers'.

It was a tough environment, a harsh drought and I did not share much in common with the majority of the club members present. Sheard auctioneers were the preferred chant in this neck of the woods.

It's the morning of the sale! There's an ill wind blowing. I've been in better spaces. Last night the cattle handling staff tore into each other, violence and intimidation greeted me this morning. Some departed, wounded and drunk. The show must go on. I need to pull this off! The toxic vultures in the club are already circling.

A regal looking gentleman with a wide brimmed veld hat and 'stature' stick is inspecting each prepared lot rather intently. I need to bring this chap into the fold! "Morning Chief!" I smile a greeting at the portly face, framed by the hat of cattle confidence.

Casually leaning on his 'kierie' he looks at me. "How do you address me as Chief, when you do not know me..!?" the righteous retorted. He draws himself up to full height. "Oh God, Hutchinson, just dig yourself deeper into the shit, in this armpit of existence," I whisper out the corner of my grim smile - to no one in particular.

Turning to face 'Chief', I reply, "You look like a Chief! And you are looking at all the best cattle!" A wide grin breaks out on his 'chops'. "Hau! Are you the auctioneer?" I reply with measured enthusiasm that I might be ... "Well I am the Chief!" he responds ... For years after that I only ever knew him as Chief.

It's showtime, Obelix picks up on my vibe. "Are we going to be OK, Hutch? There are only twenty buyers' cards issued and half are tyre kickers." I calm the waters with steely determination - "Watch me pull a rabbit out of a hat today, my man!" We get Maverick to jockey all the heifer lots, the Chief gets a few and the governmental buyers clean up the stud section of the sale. We crawl our way out of the morass that is - The East Cape Nguni club sale.

12
STANDERTON

There is not a lot that I am entirely convinced of in this world. Facades are plentiful, cameras lie and nothing is as it seems. However, I am without doubt as to the existence of two opposing forces within this life. Good and evil.

I have encountered evil, where the smell of it is palpable and the taste of it like a fetid rumour on the rise! Once, in a totally unrelated space to the settings of this book ... and the other being - Standerton stockyard. This auction venue has four auction rings right next to one another and a 'super bowl' of buyers!

As a buyer, you may bid on all four sales rings simultaneously! An auctioneer has to be on top of his game in this house!! Dropping the bid or miss calling a bid in this fast track scenario is not an option - you will end up a bonded slave to the house!

To the untrained eye, or 'Joe Soap', this place reeks of excitement, riches and opportunity. The thing is ... it is all of that ... The house is governed by a slithering undercurrent of greed, betrayal and latent criminality. The excitement, the chase and buying battles amongst the guests at this 'Hotel California' are hectic, all the while shepherded by the 'gunners' on the gavels.

Large sums of money are at stake on each lot - ethics and truth are always going to be marginal attendees at this soirée.

Razzmatazz, 'the getting, not the having' and bottom line greed motivate attendance at these mass gatherings of the Cluedo Kings as they 'stab each other with their steely knives'.

Immerse yourself in a barrage of bellowing cattle, whistles, shouts from stock handlers, banging and clanging of metal gates, the constant murmur of human voices, shouts of confirmation from bid spotters and three other auctioneers trying to capitalise on attracting buyers away from your ring! Everyone in the house is chasing the big money bids.

Each auctioneer is riding the coattails of the devil. Bids get pulled out the air, bids are called short, in favour of a quick knock to a favoured buyer. Bid increments run up the ladder like 'Jack' and they most definitely use the house as a ghost buyer - buyer no 99.

How the hell did I arrive at this junction ...? Anyway, I'm on the podium in this 'Hotel California'. Fifty twitching Brahman heifers bottleneck the entrance to the ring; jostling, jumping and riding each other's backs, with deep throated bawling amplifying their presence in the ring. My weight guesstimate alludes to two hundred twenty kilograms and I draw attention to their empty status - "Hulle is leeg manne", close to true weight! No feed or water in their bellies to diminish the per kg price on the hoof.

They are packed like sardines in a tin, heads sticking out over the next one's shoulder - they stand tightly bunched in the metallic cage. Two hundred twenty kilograms flashes red on the digital scale! With no scale at Manley Flats – my eye is trained! I know I have the best offering between the auctioneers right now! I delay my opening bid... Where's my insurance policy? There he is! 'Burger Boy' is stationed at the foot of the podium, munching on the burger I bought him just now. My new 'best friend' is eager to please.

A change in auctioneers is much the same as a change in umpires on the cricket field ... all the players try it on. I take over from the outgoing auctioneer and even with the fantastic offering in my ring, the buyers' attention migrates to the competing 'gunners' next to me.

Driving down my opening bid, they try to derail my lot and claw the calves away for as little as possible. They didn't count on the Burger Boy; he jumps right in and pumps his signal! He's loud and proud! Remember ... perception is everything. He is playing the game and loving the limelight ... never mind the burger.

One buyer, then the next, then the next dribble back into the

game. I have their interest and there is no further use for 'Burger Boy' but I give him a few short knocks on single unit lots and he is on my side. The day is long, loud and tests my ethics on each and every lot. I'm convinced of the forces at play, I do not doubt the devil is in the house.

Back in the Eastern Cape and the call comes through. I attend the meeting in Port Elizabeth and the 'Boss' of the yard requests that I join the party up north. I politely declined, citing my voice would not hold out. There are no microphones for auctioneers in Standerton. The real reason was ... I just couldn't dance with the devil. I checked out of 'Hotel California' and did manage to leave.

13

MERCY, MERCY

Some properties just change hands at a slower pace than others ... especially if the property in question happens to be agricultural ground falling inside a rain shadow area. This place had seen it all - public auction, silent tender, offer to purchase formats, all to no avail.

We decided to canvass across the hunting outfitters and in particular, those outfitters hosting clients from Scandinavian origins. It wasn't long and we had an interested party. I had to be out of town on the pre-arranged weekend of viewing and handed over the reins to 'The Operator'. For whatever reason he fails to make the allotted appointment at this remote property. 'The Viking' accompanied by his professional hunter/chaperone, somehow gains access to the property and they proceed without 'The Operator' in attendance.

At this time the region is in the grip of a deathly drought! The Spekboom and 'Witgat' trees are stunted and have no plans for growth or leaf production. Every form of browse is playing 'Jeckel & Hyde', trying to stave off the relentless fireball in the sky and the total onslaught from desperately grabbing tongues of the herds of Kudu. This property has an over-abundance of the species. Distress fire wires between the living plants! (Yes ... plants do communicate). The Kudu browse pattern is hammering the retarded foliage. All the remaining fetters of food dispatch survival code amongst themselves. Tannin production becomes an industrial exercise for the biome, trying to survive on this overpopulated patch of Africa. The tannin factories deter the hungry Kudu and browsing decreases ... as does the affected Kudu population ... Starvation becomes a reality. The tannins are taking over!

Now, I am sure, you are asking ... "Why don't the animals just move to another browse pantry?" Well, a big, fuck-off game fence might just represent a challenge if you happen to be an herbivore confined to a finite area.

Fences preserve ... Humans either conserve or consume that which is placed behind a barrier. The original intention to preserve has to be diluted, as time passes, and the preserved lives become a multiplied population. The bottom line is, if you fence off an area, restricting natural movement of livestock and wildlife, you better be prepared to manage/control the lives within this finite feeding zone.

CAE - Certificate of Adequate Enclosure! This represents the holy grail of government approval for the liquidation or cultivation of wildlife on a property that is adequately fenced and duly inspected by nature conservation officials. Landowners may farm, harvest, capture and relocate wildlife to other properties with a CAE. In essence, this sounds like a magnificent conservation plan for South Africa's wildlife! In most instances it is! However, all the best laid plans in the world have their pitfalls. In this case, absentee landlords represent a problem for growing wildlife populations behind the fences.

Africa! And the hunt, flicker framed the anticipation of the coming days. Blue skies, rolling savannah lands, foothills and towering mountain ranges stood guard over the ancient land. Big, thick necked, swarthy Kudu bulls, gracious Impala, boisterous Zebra and endless herds of Blesbok and Wildebeest, all championed for a cognitive journey in The Viking's mind … But there was always the Kudu! He was to hunt Kudu and pigs on this safari. It was a long flight from Oslo.

The gate closed behind The Viking and the professional hunter, acting as his chaperone. The Nordic adventurer was to view the property only … one would have thought that his hunting rifle would have remained safely stowed in its travel case! I never did ascertain the identity of the chaperone. I do believe that was probably for the best.

The dehydrated, tannin laden Spekboom, was pale and insipid, tailored in a 'jacket of drought'.

The usual clustered stands of sweet grasses were conspicuous in their absence, decimated by the reaching teeth of the bolstered herbivore populations on the property. This patch of Africa straddled dry, clay-caked topography, interspersed with outcrops of shale, creating a false Karoo biome. This transitional landscape surrounded The Viking and his chaperone as they penetrated the property. Picture this farm as a series of horseshoe shaped dry riverbeds; deep, wide kloofs and pinnacles of cliff faces reaching skywards above the dry water courses. Fantastic vantage points over the arid landscape stretched and bent along the seasonal, switch backed drainage line.

Here, the Kudu run like 'rats'. The bulls are 'skelm', but the cows and calves are thick amongst the stunted vegetation. They appear larger than their actual physical being. Herds run ahead of the vehicle noise, swarming around the decimated stands of sparse browse material. Some stumble, weak and thin, their guts bloated by excessive tannin consumption. The accelerated heart rates and pumping adrenaline push the poison hard.

The first bullet smashes across the far side of the kloof. A siren of consequence begins its rollercoaster ride along the perfectly machined grooves in the hunting rifle barrel. As the projectile screams out of the muzzle breaker, there's no way to retrieve the fired round and the advanced litany of lead drops the first cow in her tracks. Regardless of the consequences, The Viking's trigger finger finds relief and the lead continues to fly. Spent cartridges are ejected in rapid succession from the rapid fire 'Valkyrie'. The Viking commands this angel of engineered death, allowing her a presumptuous bounty. The chaperone is silent. The rifle bolt works overtime and death visits the Kudu herd. Kudu carcasses lie strewn about on the opposite hillside. Pools of red soak into the soil around the euthanized creatures.

The crashing sound of consequence reverberates down the kloofs and dissipates in the thorn tree-lined riverbed. The consequence of these 'mercy killings' by The Viking starts to converge at my door. The footfalls of blame consolidate to conspire against me, as The Viking exceeds his welcome and crosses the line.

The following day breaks to my client's farm shed, housing a plethora of Kudu carcasses swinging on meat hooks.

The Operator arrives after The Viking concludes a little stroll down the riverbed in front of the homestead. To those of you not well versed in identifying African antelope, Kudu and Nyala females are collectively termed as cows ... however, that's the sum total of similarity between the species. Kudu are much bigger in body, longer on the leg and have oversized radar dishes as ears. Kudu generally have a different style of coat, in colour and weave. The other pertinent fact is that hand-raised Nyala command a tidy sum on wildlife auctions ... surely a seasoned hunter would know this? At any rate, that morning, the tame, hand-raised Nyala cow, belonging to my client's daughter, was summarily dispatched by The Viking.

The Operator festoons his phone call with delicately placed positives and lightly veiled descriptions of the carnage. It's a fairly long telephone exchange. I'm not left with any confidence as to my longevity and any kind of forward placed guarantee of a life!

My client is rumoured to have links to Mossad (we all know who those guys are ...). The following days are consumed by hastily convened meetings, multiple cell phone collaborations and various attempts to smooth the waters, so to speak ...

Eventually, matters come to a head and the letter of demand lands on my desk. Reparations are sought! I take note of the bottom line figure - there's a ... one ... followed by a ... two ... and a shitload of zeros before the sequential point and the balance of zeros. The invoice is made out to ... yours truly. Holy crap!

The Viking has departed for Scandi via OR Tambo airport and I'm left carrying the can. My client calls ... and I answer. "Hutch, I will lock your client down at OR Tambo if that cash is not in my account by 4pm today." The man's position is clear.

The Operator, the hunting outfitter and I gather our collective wits about us. Somehow the small fortune is paid and The Viking passes through OR Tambo, unfettered.

Although the cash is paid, tensions remain and the Viking's offer of ten million rand for fifty per cent of the property is rejected by my client ... you win some, you lose some.

14

COWBOYS ON THE COLLECTIVE

The sudden growth in the game capture/relocation industry between 2009 and 2017 inspired and attracted a multitude of ambitious helicopter pilots. Newbies with enough hours logged to get themselves killed in a fast moving, mass capture situation, through to old bush pilots who knew how to put a machine through its paces. Most 'fly boys' pushed the envelope, and a few paid the ultimate price.

Robinson 22 and Robinson 44 choppers were mostly in evidence. Occasionally a Bell jet ranger would make an appearance. Flying in a Robby at low altitude, with the doors off, motivating a herd of Blesbok towards the capture curtain at full pace is pure adrenalin! The other capture technique used on plains game - net gunning - definitely requires supreme skill and communication between pilot and gunner. This technique allows selective capture, however there are inherent dangers associated with this capture method. The net must be meticulously packed into the release funnel to avoid an unbalanced release and bad spread of the weighted capture device. An incorrectly discharged net can easily end up in the tail rotor blade of the machine, resulting in an untimely meeting with mother earth. Chemical darting of game from a helicopter is more tactical and usually done at slower airspeed ... Nevertheless, here we are swooping down upon a pod of colour variant Blesbok as they seek to escape the clatter of the whirlybird honing in on them. The animals lengthen their stride in a bid to shake the pest descending onto their line of escape. We are about 5 metres off the deck, with 'Dr Slick' leaning out the back of the '44 desperately looking to place his dart into the rump of the ewe bringing up the rear. I take note of the fast approaching Wattle plantation and the outstretched fingers of the forest. Our Captain pumps the foot controls and manipulates the collective with precise skill. The flying bubble pivots, swings and flares within the judgement arena of Captain's peripheral vision - what a pilot! We darted the bounty and enjoyed success on the day, walking away intact from a highly dangerous endeavour.

After each auction, capture plans and logistics became the order of the day - The KZN 'fly boys' came down to assist with a capture in the Anne's Villa area. 'Asterix' could fly and his engineer, a large fellow with a primal beard, ginger in colour. was more than handy with a net gun. We could hear the chopper but it remained unseen. Our party was parked atop a cliff face surveying the floodplain below for Bushbuck, Duikers and Steenbok. Over the next few days, the 'fly boys' were tasked with net gunning all three species in numbers. *WHUPPA, WHUPPA, WHUPPA,* the rotor blades laboured as they challenged the air particles with Asterix needling the Robby out of the riverine foliage, heading for altitude. Rotor wash bent the acacia thorn trees at obscure angles and chased up a dust cloud in the dry riverbed. We had located the intrepid duo. The engineer was suspended outside the cabin, with both feet on the strut as Asterix catapulted the bird past our vantage point. These operators were at one with their machine. I personally made a mental note not to fly with them - three's a crowd.

Each Steenbok was meticulously blindfolded, sedated and placed in separate holding crates as the chopper flew the captured animals in to the receiving station. As far as I know, this was the most focused Steenbok relocation operation in the Eastern Cape at the time. As the auctioneer, I tried to be involved or attend most of the capture sites for all the game we auctioned off. All in all, I got to fly in my fair share of choppers in a range of topographies and weather conditions. On a Sunday morning I found myself in a Robinson 44 with three other large fellows ... that's four big guys in a Robby 44 with a flight plan beyond the Zuurberg mountain range. I sat upfront with the pilot. While the pilot ran through the checks and procedures, I politely enquired as to our weight-to-lift ratio ...? "No problem", was the reply. Well, we had to effect a low, extended take off, while the turbine and rotors tortured the metal frame and all the rivets, tasked with keeping the flying machine whole. We shuddered, shook and rattled ... struggling to realise the lift we needed.

So ... Robinson helicopters are known to fall out of the sky during low-G flight conditions. The Robinson operates with a semi-rigid two bladed rotor system that can lead to mast bumping, resulting in the chopper breaking up during flight. So here we are, in an overloaded R44 in a low-G flight with a pilot suffering from acute arrogance or 'Ostrich Syndrome' (head stuck in the sand), a known South African condition!

The bird clears the N2 dual carriageway, negotiates space under overhead wires and the pilot manages to find spatial purchase in a positive up draught. My headset quashes out the sound of the rotor blades as they impersonate boomerangs, flicking past the bubble canopy ... Three words form large capital imprints on my frontal lobe - "MY FOK MENSE".

The Zuurberg mountain range escalates into view and the altimeter suggests we won't clear the granite outcrops! A big male baboon challenges the metallic dragonfly as the skids pass over his troop, throwing the scattering of apes into an unnatural disco of flickering shadow! I see his bared incisors, wicked, long pieces of ivory as if on parade, flashing bright between the rotor flickers. The crests of the first granite outcrops fall away into dramatic dungeons of remnant montane forest. A beautiful picture of untouched Tarzan-style grooves of pure wilderness. Huge Yellowwood trees with gargantuan canopies thrust above the deep shadows and tangled forest ceiling. Old man's beard coat-hangers off of the outstretched limbs of these ancient arboreal treasures. The air plants range in colour from deep mauve through mustard, yellow and sea grass greens. These calderas of refuge are left behind as the pilot banks and pivots, seeking a tentative set down of the chopper in the dry riverbed at Kudus Kloof.

The darting of the Buffalo bull is carried out and all vital stats collated for the upcoming auction. By the time 'Dr Herriot' has packed up, the air temp in the Baviaans valley has risen considerably. Due to the heat, we enjoy a snooze and leak adrenalin while we wait for the heat to dissipate. Our bumble bee chariot of the skies just won't handle the depleted air particles and discretion is the better part of valour.

15

THE HOUSE OF ORANGE

Graaff-Reinet is a quaint Eastern Cape Town in the Great Karoo. Well maintained properties with tree-lined avenues and the aroma of wealth. Wildlife refuges, hideaways and reserves are plentiful, as they range across the mountains around the town.

Old money controls the municipality and everything works. An Eastern Cape anomaly! Personalities abound and foreign currency underwrites the sophisticated land barons in this neck of the woods.

Buffalo, Lechwe, Sable, Giraffe, Rhino, big cats! - You name it, these conservation-oriented business people breed with and trade all of the above ... plus more. Take a species such as Scimitar Horned Oryx (my personal favourite). Permits to capture and transport this species are nigh on impossible to achieve, but if you look carefully, there they are ... to be found in large herds roaming free. Common plains game is plentiful across the expanse of private land. Our country's heritage rests easy with these wildlife custodians.

High up in the mountains, North East of this Karoo gem, is a property owned by The House of Orange - Dutch royalty of some sort. I came to be involved with marketing their surplus game by means of auction; Black Wildebeest, Blesbok, Mountain Reedbuck and springbok. The black wildebeest went very well at the Graeme College game sale while the rest of the offering fell into place with respectable bids achieved.

Standing in the farmhouse, nursing a six a.m. coffee, I am feeling pretty relaxed looking forward to the new day. Yesterday's capture had gone well enough and a truck and trailer full of Blesbok had made passage to Grahamstown last eve.

My hands cup around the welcome warmth and my fingers feel at home. "Weasel" and I chat freely while the 'lieutenants' of the capture teams make ready to leave. We have more Blesbok on the agenda today and judging by yesterday, we should finish up the Blesbok capture this afternoon.

While I'm chatting to Weasel I detect a slight nervousness around his demeanour ... "Probably just nervous about today," I think to myself. The extra long drag on his cigarette, a shift of the eyebrows and a bit of a twitch, all send a pulse of an amber light to me while we shoot the breeze.

Weasel looks uncomfortable and I start to feel the way he looks ... "Interesting this interaction." ... His phone rings. Weasel answers the call. The conversation is limited with Weasel ejecting a few surprised comments from a tight-lipped mouth. Something is up! Suddenly the coffee doesn't taste that great anymore, the long life milk and the excessive sugar coming out of hiding. I watch Weasel as he ends the call ... "How many?" I ask. Weasel looks at me over his spectacles, mouth see-sawing, a slight stutter producing a stilted response ... "Fif ... fift ...y" - "plus ...mi ...nus."

The coffee really tastes kak now! "Are you kidding?" "No sir!" Weasel expels with conviction. "Are you fuckin' kidding me?" I reiterate. There comes a lengthy silence between us, my finger tapping on the side of the coffee cup. A gentle mountain breeze swishes through the stand of Cypress pines next to the house ... While we size each other up, the Robby 22 comes to life with a throaty roar. Weasel wishes to acknowledge the dead blesbok as an inconvenient truth and I just want to rip his head off!

We are two hundred fifty kilometres from the bomas and our flight pattern is full for the day; chopper hours are booked! How the hell will I ever actually confirm this report ... ? "Hutchinson, you've just been had! BAM!" That's all that pins my ears back as I look at Weasel. 'The feel-good factor' runs away with its tail between its legs.

The balance of this day was a blur; herds of Blesbok, dust storms from stampeding hooves, half-baked capture bomas and a dismal result, will render the picture for you.

Mass capture wasn't working on this property, the first day's catch had made the rest of the animals 'wise'. The first capture had been a 'flash in the pan' - a very expensive one at that!

The balance of the auction sales had yet to be caught and the buyers were waiting. A few phone calls from a coffee shop in town and a three man, well, two men and one lady team were on their way! I packed Weasel off and stayed on the property waiting for the net gunners to arrive. 'The Nephew' joined me with his truck and the second half was about to start ...

The bird arrived on a trailer late that day, so we arranged for an early morning recce flight. The evening was spent making the nets ready and checking equipment while going over the receiving plan.

This team turned out to be rather impressive! Absolute 'diamonds in the rough'. The pilot was extremely aware of altitude, temperature and the measured wind speeds! For a young pilot, he was meticulous in his approach to the machine and the loose bits of capture equipment, such as the packing of the capture nets into the funnels. The gunner was fearless, engrossed in obtaining the prize! And their lady ground crew component was a logistics 'major' - professional, totally professional!

Not one mortality was suffered and the auctioned animals were steadily netted, loaded and tranquilised. I managed to regain some sort of cheer, especially when the trust account started paying out and I could nurse my financial scratches and scrapes! "Elke sport het sy beserings!"

The black wildebeest bulls off this property were of an above average quality and besides the auctions, out of hand sales required extended operations here.

The Karoo vegetation is interesting! These wide open expanses can seem like a desert, yet, diverse succulents and sporadic grass cycles carpet the soil, yielding quality sustenance for herbivores. I could only imagine what the interior of Southern Africa looked like before the arrival of goats and sheep.

As I spent more time in these mountains, I accumulated pools of respect for the generations of South Africans that farmed, fought battles, hid from the law, settled, and or traversed this landscape. The rough landscape of craggy amphitheatres, koppies and mountains, the weather and the pendulum like temperature changes would most certainly have moulded and tempered any man's endeavours here.

The descriptive term, indigenous, best describes the path to sustainability in this environment. Sustainability is further brought into question by range and is ultimately governed by human greed. Greed is unknown to four legged creatures; they use what they need, or that which is available to them inside of a fenced area.

Plant matter morphs into animal genes and animal genes are manipulated into currency, which for the most part are reemployed into animal genetics. Human greed then re-populates the finite range with ... increased mouths on the matter - for financial gain. Hereby challenging the plant biomass and challenging the sustainability of the animal husbandry project. All of the above had been the common practice on this property before 'The House of Orange'.

The custodian of the farm was pertinent as to the mouths that were on the veld and I was witness to the test camps of rested Karoo veld ... what it could look like!

The capture operation ceases and my attentions are diverted to the lowveld. I am canvassing for a possible auction up north! In between different flights, my office assistant starts badgering me to pay over the last monies for game captured with The House of Orange ... twenty seven thousand rand ... To appease the admin attack, I push the buttons and make the payment. Two weeks later, the royal custodian calls, gently enquiring as to when I will make the balance of payment. Alarm bells peal out and I chase back to the office. Yip, I've been conned! The email received into our office requesting payment into the nominated account doesn't look kosher ... Not long after that, the assistant relocates to another city and the SAPS enquiries fizzle out when their leads dry up.

Karma is a bitch and I can only hope she bites hard in this regard!

I always used to think - "The future is bright ... The future is orange." Orange is no longer my colour ...

16

'FAT-BOY-SLIM'

During the eighties, Adrian Nieuwoudt swindled many a hopeful South African out of their finances. People paid five hundred rand for milk culture … a culture of repetition …

What was that all about? Desperation, gullibility or that age-old attraction of hope! Conmen weave a web and they do it well! In the end, they manage to weave unwitting people into their web and draw off those resources to further their own end. 'Fat-Boy- Slim' was a master weaver of the web …

Smoke and mirrors work well for magicians; these props deceive or confuse the less attentive members of their audience. Conmen and swindlers operate on a much larger stage! These operators have props and special effects that defy the imagination. Their influence and manipulation is subtle, while their incorporation of the subject's resources completes their objective.

Fat-Boy-Slim had a couple of objectives to achieve, if he was to continue swimming through the shark infested waters he had chosen in which to immerse himself. These included: buying time - creating paper wealth towards advancing creditors - social climbing and then the gifting … always the gifting. Appeasing and creating promise amongst those hounding for remuneration or compensation.

I came to know Fat-Boy-Slim through cattle and goat dealings. These were reasonable out of hand deals, with one or two auction appearances.

On my various visits to his property, I noticed small herds of Impala, Springbok, Blesbok and a couple of giraffes. By the time we extended business to include wildlife, Fat-Boy-Slim had an enthusiastic auctioneer in his arsenal of stage props.

In his soft and gentle manner, Fat-Boy-Slim enquiries as to my latest auction prices on a few different species and if I can email these to him. A few days later, it's Fat-Boy-Slim on the line again - "Do you have a pen and paper handy?" he asks ... I start writing down the species and numbers he is committing to the next auction. On the final tally, over one hundred head of game animals. Kudu bulls and cows, springbok, impala, and gemsbok! A fantastic entry! All off one capture zone! This is a great anchor to the upcoming sale. The kudu and the gemsbok would fly and the other plains game would be snaffled up at hunting market prices - the bread and butter finances of my auction were confirmed. I secured a few other high end submissions of bontebok and buffalo; these were welcome additions to a grand offering of wildlife! I was convinced this was to be a fantastic date on my auction calendar.

On the day of the sale, the high end animals are structured throughout the early stages of the lots, creating the energy that would lift the common species bids skywards!

A grand entry of Bontebok from 'Marathon Man' raced up the value chain, topping out close to one hundred thousand rand for ewes. The seller was all smiles! Buffalo bulls went for market related prices and a few heifers went unsold - TBC (To Be Confirmed). The balance of the sale rests squarely with Fat-Boy-Slim's entry. The Gemsbok are first up! It's a scramble of bids and the desert antelope ratchet up their rand value from opening bids of five thousand rand to nine thousand rand, resulting in a twenty per cent surplus on the reserve price! The bontebok, buffalo and gemsbok lots begin to let me feel like the comic book character - 'Richie Rich'. A couple of million rand in turnover and yours truly is the toast of the day with sellers clambering to offer thirst quenching thank you gifts and to firm up capture dates.

In amongst the auction attendees, I take note of a few serious 'Buffalo Boys'. They just came to pencil in the catalogue prices ... finding their benchmark pricing. This is Lower Albany - a fickle mixture of Settlers and Nuevo rich game farmers.

The springbok performed well on the sale and I plan the opening capture logistics around Fat-Boy-Slim's entry, starting with the springbok.

The morning of the capture arrives. Picture a convoy of vehicles; eight ton trucks, utility vehicles with trailers, smaller transport trucks and various buyers' vehicles. The buyers have come to observe their animals being loaded. This is a large PR event, a showcase of our expertise and commitment! The chopper is already on the property and the pilot has his instructions - "Upon sight of the convoy, fly out of the sun, over the length of the vehicles, bank and fly back, past the front to the rear of the approaching line of vehicles (watch for wires!)" The pilot outdoes himself and the show starts with the Robinson doing a low level buzz of the buyers! "Well done," I smile.

The capture team gets busy building the boma and I instruct the pilot to swing a grid pattern over the property, to locate the springbok herds and get a rough idea of the balance of the expected game numbers ... "Let's just say ... If you are aiming to catch fifty springboks, you need to have a hundred available ... If you catch forty impala, you better have an option of driving a hundred twenty towards the capture boma ... etc. I trust you get the picture?"

The pilot has the chopper in a grid system flying at slow airspeed. As I observe the bird, the pilot doubles back, then scoots off here, then there - breaking the grid. "That's a little out of sorts," I think to myself. I don't have radio comms with the pilot and wait for his return. The pilot doubles up on his trot away from the downward curved rotor blades. He has returned quicker than expected ... "Boss, there are no large herds on this property!" "Boskak! Man, what are you telling me?" I'm not in the mood for bullshit jokes! The clock is ticking and expectations are high. "No jokes," says the aviator. The chopper's rotors are slowly coming to a standstill behind us. A margin call is needed! - pack up and leave or catch what we can to salvage something out of this 'pig's ear' of a PR exercise.

The sun is climbing and the shadows shift, as the fingers of the fireball creep across the crisp morning veld.

Weasel is in for a penny, in for a pound and either way, I'm paying. He takes on the filter end of the tungsten tobacco stick, exhaling lazy, full blue smoke rings into the dying wash of the chopper's rotors.

The decision is consummated - fly the bird, carry on with the show and bring in as many Springbok as possible on the first push! Let's get the spectators away as soon as possible.

"You got it, Boss," and with that, both Weasel and the pilot make for the sky, tossing me a radio as they depart. The chopper rattles and hums with the rotor blades adding the single beat bass to the early morning atmosphere. An atmosphere of expectation and hidden tension! "Please let them bring something in ..." I plead to the still morning air.

Weasel and the pilot are chatting freely over the frequency, their banter doesn't translate into good business. "Bring that parcel of springbok in!" I interject, disturbing their tea party.

The earlier vibe of the capture operation is wearing off amongst the buyers ... now it's becoming, "Where the animals, Hutch?"

I watch the chopper dip below the first horizon as it fiddles along, finding a batch of buck. Eventually a smallish mish-mash of pronking springbok appear amongst the Witgat trees. The chopper hangs back, shepherding the group, keeping the stragglers and scatterings closed up for the boma approach. The group needs a hard push now to cross the curtain wire ... "WeeeweeeeeWeee" goes the siren on the bird and the pilot roughnecks the chopper down onto the sprinting antelope. With elongated strides and lolling tongues, the pilot races them over the wire and the curtain closes! "Wee wee," and the siren confirms the capture! The chopper secures its zenith over my position and I salute the pilot - a signal of thanks!

We process this bunch of animals and dispatch the waiting buyers with quarter and half loads ... providing promise of the balance of the buck later on.

The pressure subsides and it's time for me to get a first-hand look at my exposure on this property. Thirty minutes later and I am in no doubt as to the deception placed at my door. The ratios and population of animals are a misnomer. I will do well if I come out of this financially intact.

Fat-Boy-Slim arrives – astride of his four wheeler. He is happy to see Springbok being loaded. I approach the spring-weary chariot, requesting a quick chat. For a rather large Afrikaner male, Fat-Boy-Slim had an almost angelic, soft-n-sweet vocal cue. "I mean, butter wouldn't melt on his tongue." I don't mince my words. After I've finished communicating my concerns, he replies, "Your pilot must have chased all the animals through the fence to my neighbour ... Who's paying for that?" The sweet, melodic tone from the overly large man belies the latent intent. He guns the quad bike motor and makes for the comfort of his homestead. The fading quad bike motor allows me space to verbalise instructions. "Catch what you can!"

Later in the day, Fat-Boy-Slim arrives with a legal practitioner. The legal eagle starts laying claim to the kudu, gemsbok and a few other bits 'n pieces of game still in the holding trucks.

Fat-Boy-Slim owes this guy money for legal representation. The only means of payment that can be presented by Fat-Boy-Slim ... is the wildlife incarcerated in the holding trucks.

The angelic voice pleads with me to release the animals into the lawyer's care ... promising me better deals on cattle and hinting at some massive property deal ... etc. Fat-Boy-Slim is at his wits end. I sat there in the veld, holding this man's future in the palm of my hand. After some careful consideration, I grant the lawyer the kudu and ease the big man's precarious situation. In doing so, I gathered another client and spared Fat-Boy-Slim from stumbling onto the legal man's chopping block.

I managed to just cover costs and moved onto another property in the area to provide the impala and springbok needed. Luckily the gemsbok carried the operational costs on this day! We returned to the farm at a later stage and topped up on kudu while catching bushbuck, duiker and steenbok.

I wonder if this chap managed to extract himself from the clutches of the legal leviathan or if the sharky waters finally took their toll?

17

'COMRADE'

Hushed tones of … "Huuutch … Huuutch" consolidate in my ear piece. Whispered calls of my nickname, softly drawn out, late at night … "Mmmm" … Xi xom xa! (hier kom kak)

I listen to the urgent whisperings and start planning an escape route for my besieged friend. The distressed whispers relay a complete 'cluster fuck' of a situation. An unbelievable cloak of badness stalked my friend, at this late hour.

Death and damage floated free on the night airs … Valkyries had made their selection.

"He is dead, Hutch!" 'Comrade' stutters 'n splutters over the line …

An expired, unknown member of a local community lies dead in the capture teams' accommodation. The balance of the bullshit is laid bare by Comrade as he spills the beans … "Bra!" He excitedly, half whispers, "this chopper got here just before dark, and now the pilot is pissed … and I've got this dead man, and the capture team are also pissed." Comrade is wallowing in a quagmire of 'cowboy kak'.

Comrade needs to disassociate himself from 'a dead man walking', the pissed pilot and the menagerie of ground crew he has assembled! I start putting two and two together … A fugitive airman, pissing it up on arrival, a ground crew equally inebriated and congruous … mmmm. I hazard a guess as to the identities of Comrade's capture crew - 'Oubaas' and 'Kaz' … "Are those two your go-to team, Comrade?" Jesus, I can't believe it! Comrade has bewildered me. Now, Oubaas is a particularly good pilot, but his legitimacy with the South African aviation authorities is less than limited and his bird has a questionable certificate of fitness, never mind ownership issues. Oubaas is enslaved to the goose neck bottle of amber liquid that he secretes in his upper vest pocket. This gentleman is in short, a liquor-swigging, 'cowboy on the collective'. A true gunslinger of the skies.

"Load up that dead man and take him to the closest clinic." I advise Comrade. "Get him gone! Can you hear me, Comrade?" I enquire down the crackling cyber line. In the background, I make out the familiar drawl of Kaz.

Kaz has a distinctive lower Albany 'boet 'n swaer' slow style language, monopolised by much punctuation! And quiet power words. However … when the brandy breaks out, it becomes loud and loaded, leading the company a merry dance! Between Oubaas and Kaz, the party starts cranking in the background. The phone is massaged out of Comrade's grip and the line is hostage to the party. I think I hear … "OK, Hutch," from Comrade. Now he's on his own and the sun will be up shortly.

Early the next morning … *Brrrr whrrrr, brrr whhrrr* my phone vibrates on the kitchen table … VIDEO content … No footage of the dead man's disposal … The video shows the chopper starting up. Deep throaty exhaust, screeching belts, the rotor blades build momentum to full budget. The canopy bubble of the Robby twenty-two shimmers, shakes and vibrates. The turbine sends energy, delivering pulses throughout the bird's construction. The chopper builds to full power and the chopper skids tentatively, seeking to debrief and find the sky. OMG! Comrade is actually employing this aircraft!? I watch the video feed as Oubaas flies his grid, finding the game and testing the altitude to lift the ratio of his second string machine. "Rather him than me," I text to Comrade. "And rather you than me ... later today!"

The next video link brings visuals of a lethargic ground team building a capture boma - broken nets, bent poles, slack ground wires etc ... "Ek sê maar fokol!" Comrade continues to run with the foxes and hunt with the hounds! Although I'm not on site, I pick up the regular video feeds from Comrade. Funny that ... for two weeks after the Parks Board pitch, I had heard nothing from this quarter. now it's like I'm part of a reality TV show ... let's call it ... 'Kill 'em quick town'.

Every passing minute, Comrade is sinking and sinking fast into the 'cowboy kak' - not even a snorkel is going to help him!

Video feeds show herds of black wildebeest charging down mountainsides, Oubaas working miracles at high altitude, only to lose the animals to poorly constructed capture bomas and poor communication on the ground. By midday, the capture bomas and trucks stand empty ... and the unpredictable mountain air starts mutating into a thin-lipped viper. Sharp needles of lightning perforate the high mountain atmosphere. Comrade is leaning dangerously close to the financial abyss yawning before him. I can't take it anymore. I call his number and he answers ... "Comrade, ditch this crew! Stop this capture now! These guys couldn't give a rat's arse about whether they catch your quota or not! Come this pm, they will own you brother!" I am still sounding out my warning, when he sighs, "They are here!"... "WHO's there?" I batter the phone's earpiece with my vocality. "The Parks officials," he sighs, stress strangling his volume, and expels leftover air from his lungs as I sense that he surrenders to the situation.

"Shit Comrade, do not land that chopper! Get Oubaas out of there!" The line clicks dead, starving me of contact. I have visions of Comrade, Kaz and Oubaas being locked up and the chopper impounded. Never mind the civil action from 'Mr Bones' kraal ... (I still wonder how Comrade dodged that bullet).

Oubaas recognised the officials' vehicle as pertinent problems. He bugged out and flew, low, slow and south. The unlicensed bird was hugging the rims of river valleys, drainage lines and treetops. Helter-skelter for home! Kaz packed up his tattered capture clothes and chastened his crew to the departing truck. Comrade was left to face the music - Yodwa!

When the bird bugged out, the operation folded and Comrade was able to cite mechanical failure of the chopper as his Achilles heel. My friend dodges a dangerous enquiry from the officials. Comrade is a likeable fellow and he manages to win over the head honcho and secures a second stab at the task at hand. He convinces the park officials that mass capture is not an option in this terrain and they agree to allow him to proceed with a chemical capture operation. Comrade lives ... to fight another day!

In due course, Comrade returns to the mountains with a licensed chopper and a dependable vet. Together, they load enough black wildebeest onto the Nephew's truck to conclude a successful relocation. Comrade comes out of the experience with his underpants intact ... but the dead guy is dead and that must haunt my friend.

18

PROVIDENCE

How do we come to be in certain places, at specific times? Is our life path preordained, interlinked with others in some kind of huge celestial symphony? We all have the power to take a life, save a life or destroy the lives around us, an interchangeable power that commands respect for the balance of life. Every day we are governed by our choices ... but every so often we cross paths with beings that need assistance to be able to continue on their life path.

The chopper blades are slicing through the thin, hot air, the pilot dancing his machine around the low hills. The vast blue expanse of the Gariep dam shimmers like the Mediterranean and the heat bears down on us while we anticipate the successful darting of a bonded, breeding pair of white steenbok!

These two rare-colour variant steenbok had been snapped up on the previous catalogue game sale and now it was delivery time. This delivery rested entirely upon the chopper crew, who were dancing and flirting with the Karoo topography. The lead up to this chemical capture had been fraught with cancellations by our usual bunch of animal doctors, none of them keen to contest the open Karoo range. A rather specific double tap, of a breeding pair of antelope, no larger than a dwarf goat, is the task at hand.

Luckily the first piece of the puzzle - a seasoned pilot just happened to be a short hop away from this range. After lining the chopper up, we managed to get the attention of a lady vet in the area. Once she confirmed her availability, I arranged for the pilot to pick her up post haste!

Steenbok are finicky creatures and the chemical concoction to immobilise the diminutive buck has to be spot on. The chopper hovers and pivots, closely skirting the boulders and trees on the crocodile-like range of low hills. The chase, the ambush and the target, outmanoeuvre each other time and again. Radio transmission from the chopper to our handheld radios is intermittent and every few minutes a broken squelch of info besets the airwaves.

The machine protests as the pilot works the thin atmosphere, creating the space necessary for the dart to fly. Release of the chemical missile is a timing challenge of note! The flank of a Steenbok moving between multidirectional bucks and jumps becomes a miniscule strike picture while you are 'winging it' in an aircraft that struggles with heat and altitude - the chap on the collective has my respect!

Eventually 'Lara Croft' releases a dart successfully and the crew confirm a cutaneous hit. The orange head of the dart mechanism is bobbing and bouncing on the flank of the bounding animal. This is positive news! And I am super eager to get this rare colour variant crated and sedated. Oddly, the chopper doesn't set down a skid or land but turns and howls across the sand flats to our position. As she comes in to land, we optimistically rush forward with a stretcher and blindfolds.

Hoping we missed a quick pick up on the far side of the hills ... Lara Croft sprint - jumps from the canopy and dashes past our receiving crew - heading for her 'box of tricks' I squelch a comment to the pilot and he signals back, negative!

Lara Croft is mixing muti and clearly upping the dosage in the darts she is preparing! The lady vet works feverishly while the chopper blades chew cash with every rotation. We stay out of her way. Shortly the bird gets lift and the two are back in operation. I watch as the pilot flies the Robby, at low level across the Flats and then pulls up into a high arc over the last contact point, searching for the bounding blur of the steenbok - a complete colour variant of a snow white steenbok!

The chopper disappears over the toothy ridge of boulders and the operation is now a muddled mix of squelch on the handheld radios. The pitch and clatter of rotor blades ricochet off the topography. It's a tense affair and the receiving team are quiet, not one of us wanting to 'jinx' the capture.

Finally, the chopper banks around the far side of the hills and flies with purpose, to our position. Binoculars confirm the bounty is on board! We blindfold, crate and sedate the first of the breeding pair. The good lady grabs another batch of darts and joins the airman. Everyone's spirit is buoyed and I sense the veterinarian's relief.

The radio squelches and buzzes with excitement ... creating suspense as the low level fly boy makes his appearance. He is reaching his machine to optimum trim across the Karoo basin.

The flying dot magnifies itself as the turbine brings the second steenbok to the receiving team.

I stand in the Karoo landscape, unbelieving … I have a bonded, breeding pair of white steenbok loaded and sedated. We actually pulled this off!!

Albinos occur in nature and you can get singular - genetic, colour variant, throwback animals … But to obtain a bonded, breeding pair of white steenbok, pure as the driven snow! Not a pink nostril in evidence or a blemish on their snow white coats … Now that's something beyond special!

I had auctioned off this pair of steenbok the previous week. The catalogue game sale had gone well and these two had enjoyed star status on the bid!

A solid rand figure attached to a telephone number of zeros and an eventual numerical point had sealed the last bid and confirmed market value of these absolute anomalies.

They were headed north. The Nephew and I were an unlikely delivery team but I needed to expand my northern contacts and The Nephew … Well, he had time on his hands, a great road trip partner!

All is wrapped up at the capture site and we point the precious cargo, north, up the N1. It's not long and the Bush-telegraph high wires across the Karoo. Bids are now coming over the phone. Last week these same 'slick willies' had scoffed at the idea that these animals even existed … claiming Photoshop agents had been at work!

Tough! North we go. "Switch that thing off," I implore of my travel partner.

There is a distinct difference between game breeders and gamekeepers! We were guided into the secure breeding facility, checked and double checked, sprayed and literally searched before we were allowed to offload the incoming steenbok.

What a facility! Habitat conjured camps with security and the utmost of contrived conditions for all of Southern Africa's tiny antelope - blue duiker, red duiker, dik dik, and suni. You name it ... This chap had them in breeding pairs. On top of this I had just delivered the crown jewels of his collection! A pure white colour variant, breeding pair of steenbok!

The following day The Nephew suggested we might be in need of some R&R ... Sun City and the Lost Palace were in close proximity! That evening we managed to schmooze our way into dinner at the Palace, without a room number or reservation ... a nudge and a wink to the maitre d and we were hobnobbing it like no tomorrow. "To the Manor borne," I whispered to my associate. He raised his glass in agreement. What a dinner it was! We were careful not to overstay our welcome and made a courteous exit in the nick of time!

That afternoon had been most entertaining. The Valley of the Waves had been our serendipity, a place of pleasure and peculiarities!

The Nephew was intent on reaching the cocktail bar overlooking the waves, striding out ahead. We were passing by a colossal oval shaped swimming pool en route to the Pina

Coladas ... When something said ... "Take off your shirt." - The nephew clearly hadn't heard, he was power walking to the bar! This had to be meant for me ... So I took my shirt off and then I was persuaded into the pool. After that the magnetic messages pushed me onwards across the large egg-shaped bath. I swam breaststroke, searching against the backdrop of opulence for a clue ... A message of some sort ... Nothing came to me and the curious communications had vaped out. I reached the end of the water and slowly turned to kickoff from the side wall of the pool. Slowly frog kicking my way back, I was at a loss ... Then I heard it ... A soft *thump thump*. Not a splash, not a struggle on the surface, rather a single weight penetrating the liquid surface - much the same as a large rock slipping off a cliff into deep water.

I stopped the frog kick, treading water, and listening for more. There came no more sound. Turning back, there were no telltale ripples, no indication of anything untoward from the party people frolicking poolside. All the while, the seconds filter away ... edging up to the pool wall, I back up and scan beneath the surface, chlorine biting my eyelids. Nothing! The party people are oblivious to anything else except their ... Party. "I didn't imagine that sound and I'm not in this pool by choice," I say to myself ... Trust me; The Nephew is irrigating his tonsils with Pina Coladas and whatever else he can assimilate for pleasure! Here I am, on a wild goose chase, prompted by some magnetic force ... As I scan to the far left, on the bottom of the pool is a small dark body. Swimming down, I am not stressed, panicky or even doubtful about this action. Picking the child up, I notice how calm he is! He looks at me, as if to say ... "About bloody time mate." Upon reaching the surface I place him, standing up next to the pool. Literally at that exact moment, an adult turns around and puts a towel around the child, as if he had been standing there all the time. A couple of people on sun loungers stand up and applaud. The poolside parent doesn't give me a second look and his party moves off with the silent boy in tow.

"Well, that's that," I suppose, as I swam past the advancing lifeguard. "Don't worry," I say to him, changing to freestyle, in an effort to join The Nephew at the bee infested bar.

That boy got a second chance at life; because of two snow white steenbok ... and of course, The Nephew's penchant for Pina Coladas!

19

TICKS 'N THINGS

An auctioneer's business is always on the lookout for new venues, markets, people and of course ... New revenue! I was constantly trying to expand the sphere of influence while cornering the cash. The 'Bug bear' in this equation is the sphere of influence. The further you move out of your area, the less influential you become. Circumspection and resistance become real factors with which to contend. With reference to livestock and wildlife auctions, people problems add to the hotpot of the environment along with disease and sicknesses that may serve to scupper any sale. Ticks carry sickness such as multiple strains of heart water, as well as African and Asiatic redwater ... Amongst others!

These tiny parasites create boundaries and corridors. As a buyer you ignore these tiny creatures at your peril! An auctioneer will gladly announce the stock is from a 'virulent' heart water area! Let me tell you ... that means diddly squat. Large losses in terms of finances and livestock can be incurred by not paying attention! A tiny creature, no larger than a matchstick head holds the animal husbandry industry to ransom in Southern Africa! These critters are literally merchants of death ...

So there I was, holding an auction in a virile heart water area, ambushed by a creature, well many creatures, of comparative size with a matchstick head. A combination within this situation, of a diminished sphere of influence and a multitude of critters … it wasn't looking too good.

Auction time and I look out over the seated bunch of saboteurs. It's a hodgepodge mix of money; there are no real buyers here yet.

The ticks are real, the people are real … it's going to be a toughie; I just hope my 'Parachute' arrives! I've done my canvassing and scouting the weeks leading up to the sale, but I don't see the fruits of that effort seated before me! This is scary shit! That Parachute better arrive! This plane is about to go down. I don't panic easily, but I can tell you, on this eve, I was pretty panicky!

The setting is complete, 'bullshit bandits' fill my seats, Ticks 'n things all around and I'm in panic mode for the first time, since my baptism of fire in Cape Town - 2008.

I must say … I was at a loss as to why there was a distinct lack of East Coast operators at this sale! I was sure there would be a few operators that needed a tax break tickle! Buying wildlife on auctions is a wonderful way to build discrete cash flow that never yields a return …

The auction is set amongst large trees alongside a river, just outside of East London. My showtime platform has been immaculately attended to, beautiful lighting and the grand audio visual arrangement are impressive window dressing for this evening.

Catalogues showcasing the wildlife on offer are interspersed between the seating and tables; it truly is a wonderful setting ... Full of 'maplotters!' The background sound brings suspense to the awesome wildlife images flashing across the screen! All of this ... and not even a whiff of currency in the air. No sign of The Parachute!

"Where are the big hitters?" Obelix hears my concern, a worried look, vacant of confidence, clouds his usually cheerful mug. He sounds the bell, there's no turning back now. My P. T. Barnum's plan of a grand entrance evaporates as I cast a jaundiced eye over this collection of tyre kickers!

While I do the necessary intros and house rules, I'm breaking the doors down, running through possible remedies to what looks like a looming fiasco! It's hot under the lights and I'm pretty sure these heathens can see my unease. Not great! The auction flow is totally incorrect for the assembled 'buyers', and the results of the opening lots confirm this ... ZERO bids! Sweating now!

Jumping around in the catalogue, I mix and match the lots, trying to bring some value to the audience. As I look up from my shaking fingers, flicking over the printed pages, I see my Parachute arriving! She is accompanied by an entourage of professional hunters and Scandinavian clients. This lady operator is dressed to the nines in African safari style! Quite an entrance! The dynamic changes in an instant - I move the heart water Springbok lots forward in the roll of sale and extract the opening bid from these new arrivals. There is energy! The Springbok lots charge the venue with fear of loss as the 'Out of

Africa' entourage bid on each lot, snapping up my call to arms. A positive focus on this group ... and I might just be able to call this an auction!

Parachute plays the game and gives me the green light on just about every damn lot! My panic subsides and I get stuck in - five thousand, five on the top, go six, fetch the other five, it's going seven, get the rest, it's a flyer ... Gonna sell now!

Tiny rivulets of sweat make their way down my spine to the small of my back. At least the nervous perspiration has been replaced by the stage presence and physical parade of newfound confidence!

My end bids are falling squarely with the Parachute, she's here to buy! Wonderful stuff!! Her entourage are lapping up the show, the huge screen and choreographed sound match the catalogue of beautiful animals! I don't think these chaps have ever seen anything like this ... where they come from.

It took a monumental effort to get Parachute to the sale but now that she's here, she's giving it horns! The weekend warriors can't resist trying to outbid her, testosterone is 'magic muti' in an auctioneer's hands. She leads these buggers down the path on every lot, a real siren! I extended a little assistance ... Here and there, she has saved the sale and I'm grateful!

We are well into the back end of the sale and a parcel of Eland is receiving sporadic attention from one or two dabblers ... then Parachute picks up the reins ... She rides this lot with gusto! Her buyer signal is strong! She's going to take it!! However, there's a red-faced brandy swiller that just won't let the good lady claim this parcel ... we are well past the reserve price, at fifteen thousand, two on the top, looking for the three, gonna go four, the bid stands firm! Any further advance? The bid is with the 'redneck' ... a silence exists as the background sound guys bring the suspense, raising the bass ... I look at Parachute down an extended arm ... "Any further advance? Gimme a small one, twenty on the top?" There it is ... The bangle adorned forearm, flicks the bejewelled wrist and forefinger into an upward nuance. I take the bid, shifting the positive energy away from the redneck at that he jumps up and turns around, expecting to find a ghost bidder ... "No, my man, not tonight!" I think to myself as I stand confident. The befuddled chap stumbles away from his seat, clearly embarrassed and just wanting out! Parachute notes the entry in her catalogue as I confirm the sale.

The auction gets some kind of momentum and Parachute buys a significant number of animals. At the close of the last lot, we all head for the bar, while Obelix and the assistant attend to buyers' queries.

Well, blow me down ... As we sit in the bar one by one the punters approach and make enquiries on unsold lots. Bloody hell, we might as well have just invited people for drinks and sold them animals in-between beers! The whole auction, these guys sat on their hands, now they doing EFTs ... nuts!

Parachute makes a silent departure and exits the venue with grace. Her clients are convinced she's an African queen and as for myself ... Well, I've still got my underpants on!

20

SLOMO - SLOJO

Immediate danger speaks to your subconscious mind. Interestingly, your subconscious mind has no language centre ... Your prefrontal cortex is a slow observer of the impending disaster and becomes a confused partner as the rapidly unfolding situation befalls you.

Time dilation starts to fill in as many actions as possible. Adrenaline and epinephrine are produced and released. These chemicals become a source of energy, strength and pain camouflage. Time continues to flow at a constant rate, however your subconscious mind is commanding your conscious mind to basic instinct - fight, flight or ... surrender.

A bull giraffe's rear hoof becomes the sky! Space fills with clear and present danger! The right side foreleg of the galloping bull steeple chases over the bonnet of the land cruiser. As the foreleg stretches to infinity, the hind leg gathers itself up and my peripheral vision notes the rocking horse, elongated, stretch of the giraffe's neck ...

This animal is a contradiction in terms! Much like time dilation ... it looks slow but moves a lot faster than you think!

The sky has now become the underside of this giraffe's hoof! The handheld radio crackles and squelches with the pilot and vet jabbering away. It's all happening so quickly, yet so retarded, in relation to the seconds seeping away. Everything around me is matter of fact and there's no loss of interpretation - I am about to have my chest smashed in by the descending hoof and the gathered force of this giraffe's hindquarters!

The driver of the cruiser looks up through the windshield and he falls into shadow as the gargantuan creature blocks out the morning sun. This giraffe has a dart in its shoulder,

An orange blob of sleep sauce is working into the sprinting strides of this skyscraper of a creature. We observed the darting from a distance and then moved up into position. At that point, the darted giraffe suddenly changes direction and within seconds, time had become magnified. The radio jabbers and the cruiser revs as the flight mode of instinct grips the driver and all the colours become clear! No nuances, no subtle palettes. It's brown, orange, black, yellow and white. In this moment, my breath slows and I am in control of this involuntary action! This is the only aspect during the morning to which I may apply some sort of leverage!

The giraffe eclipses the sun and seems sure to obliterate our lives! The cabin of the Land cruiser is to become our tin can! "We are not floating free and we certainly are not David Bowie!" (Starman - David Bowie). It's death for us. The driver has a knee jerk reaction and floors the cruiser. Our increased forward motion and the downward strike of the giraffe hoof creates the smallest of opportunities and we both watch the hoof pass by the windshield as it follows the exercise of muscle and the law of gravity.

The left side of the windshield upright is grazed by the giraffe hoof and the passenger window is filled by the giraffe hind leg and the procreation end of the massive animal. As quick as the approach was, so is the passing gallop of the giraffe as it strides away from us towards the dry riverbed. The babble on the handheld radio reaches a crescendo pitch as it appeared that we were about to become human tuna. The driver and I look at each other and not a word is spoken, no expletives - none would do justice to the previous five seconds of our lives. In the meantime, the giraffe has galloped into the riverbed and has disappeared from our sight. The radio bursts back into our senses rearranging our reverie. The giraffe is down. The Robby 22 has a hovering perch over the colossus. We drive the cruiser as far as possible and then sprint down the final stretch of dry water course. The deep imprints of the giraffe hooves in the dew soaked sand, illustrate the live weight of this massive browser. The clattering rotor blades of the chopper call us to the downed animal's position. Rotor wash assaults the riverine vegetation, bending and buckling the acacia, while rumbling miniature conglomerates of coarse sand granules around the calderas of the hoof imprints.

As we approach the giraffe, we are out of breath ... and the giraffe is lying still. This is not good!! 'The Friendly Ghost' leaps on top of the giraffe ribcage and begins to squat-leap up and down on the organ protecting splices of bone. He grunts and vocalises his breath with the physical exertion. Again and again he launches and lands on the skeletal cradle. The boots and bodyweight bunch and unbunch the vital organs of the ungulate.

Time dilation takes charge once again this morning and we are locked in a capsule with the king of time! A 'force ten' rush of air somersaults along the narrow trachea, looking for the escape hatch! *WHOOOOSH, BAAAaaah* and the dead still giraffe rejoins the spinning rock - called Earth. This giraffe is not immobilised, the head pivots upwards off the sand and begins the upward strain in search of blood pressure!

Sustained blood pressure is vital for giraffes, as you can imagine …

The backup ground crew arrive, like the 'charge of the light brigade' harnesses, ropes, blindfolds and manpower swarm around the elongated goat. The scene fast forwards with many hands attaching, tensioning and testing the applied lead ropes.

The Friendly Ghost fits the blindfold over the exaggerated eyelashes belonging to the herculean captive. I am literally in awe of the preceding string of events.

We captured and relocated six giraffes on this day, a monumental effort on the part of The Friendly Ghost and his team! Giraffes were achieving between eighteen thousand rand and twenty-two thousand rand on my auctions at the time. At the end of the day, if it pays, it stays.

21

THE DART

I needed to supply a single Impala ram to a client ... one, solitary animal! A monumental pain in the arse - the cost and the difficulty involved in this task was always going to be a challenge! Impala parcels had been delivered to a client but somehow the breeding ram had expired en route. Diligence in this regard, required that I make right the loss suffered during transportation. More so out of congeniality and my commitment to the client. Buyers don't spend money where antipathy and looseness reside!

A ram is sourced on a property that would support a chemical ground capture attempt ... Note, the word ... *attempt.*

I managed to secure the services of a Grahamstown vet, not my first choice for this kind of procedure but he should be able to handle it? Always the eternal optimistic, I meet up with the animal doctor and proceed with the task at hand. Darting a ram on this property should be 'child's play' The animals are vehicle habituated and fairly approachable. I should be able to put the vet and his chemical sniper gun within fifteen to twenty metres of an impala ram within fifteen minutes. Remember, with these animal doctors ... Time is money and money is governed by the tick-tock of the clock! There are no compensation clauses for their bloopers, just the digital dance of the stopwatch.

The allotted time kicks off on a positive note - my man has prepped a few chemical immobilisation darts. That's a good sign! Locked and loaded, we scout for a likely breeding ram. Not long and I am within fifteen metres of a lone bachelor ram. A nice wide open rack with well put together strong hindquarters ... It's a go! A whisper and a nudge focus the good Doctor's attention upon the intended quarry. He squints into the scope and within a few seconds he finds the crosshairs outlined against the red tan hide of the ram's rump. I pick up the chemical dart as it tracks through the air, a mini marvel of human ingenuity! Duikers and Impala are known for evading slow moving projectiles, such as arrows and darts! The ram jumps forward but he's a second too slow ... The dart lands slap bang on his rump, the barb hooking in deep! Cautiously optimistic, I congratulate the shooter and we wait for the dart to work its magic. Well, those tick-tock moments become minutes ... The ram continues walking away from us. The ram has no reaction towards the content of the dart and eventually walks over the hill and far away ... Bugger! "What the hell?" I say to the vet, "How the hell can that be?" That ram didn't even stagger. There is no indication of a chemical release, only the initial flinch when the dart struck home. The dart is not retrievable and the Impala has done a 'Harry Houdini'. The vet suggests we try dart another ram ... Now I know how this is going to pan out!

I consult with the landowner and he gives me the green light. On closer inspection and retrospection of the darts prepared, the 'chemical character' deduces that the initial concoction might have been insufficient to render the Impala immobile. As

I said … "He's not my first choice, but he's all I've got today." I bolster his confidence and bring him onto another ram - the dart flies … and flies … into a tree! "For goodness sakes man!" I can't hold back my frustration. He actually missed this second ram from ten metres of distance. The two darts, the time and the walking Impala are having a negative effect on my bank account! I can feel the remorse from his reluctant demeanour. He doesn't want to continue but I have to have a ram by this afternoon! We discuss the options and he is lethargic in his application of the mini laboratory he has brought with him. Regret is consuming this 'chemical brother' … "Come on, we can do this! Fix your darts up and let's cruise," I say, in a fashion of camaraderie. The next ram is further off than the first two … Twenty metres out … The chemical missile sings a whistle song as it exits the barrel of the dart gun. Tracking across the open ground, I watch the darts trajectory 'like a cat on a hot tin roof' it strikes solidly into the flank of the ram. "Hell's bells!"

I give the vet a fist pump and turn back to look at the Impala. The ram takes one step, two steps and pitches over! *WHUMP!* The front shoulder connects the ground, followed by the rest of the rigour mortis beset buck! Hind legs are stiff in their upward stretch!

"Jesus! What did you put into that dart?" I ask the doctor as I exit the vehicle, making for the stricken animal. The vet sprints behind me, fumbling with sealed syringes, I turn to see where he is placed in this sense of urgency! Sprinting, fumbling, more fumbling and then both of us are upon the impala! As I grab the horns I look into the green eye of the expiring ram, out of my peripheral vision I note the vet bringing up a syringe of antidote. Flexing the Impala neck, I provide the space necessary for a good angle on the stabbing syringe, wielded by the vet. This ram is milliseconds from death! "We can't lose him!" I shout. The savage stab has placed the antidote flush into the ram's bloodstream. The vet is sweating, cursing quietly under his breath. We both know his repertoire has been a shopping trolley full of schoolboy errors.

The impala ram's mouth opens with a deep, death rasping, oxygen grasping gurgle! This guttural noise escapes from within the Impala's life-force. At first, I thought the animal was expiring! Then his eye blinks and the ears twitch! I softly poke the right orbit of the eyes and confirm the vital sign. "Thank Fuck!" The relief is magnified for both the veterinarian and myself ... I'm sure the Impala held some perspective on the situation.

The impala ram spider legs his way to full stature. Firmly gripping the woozy captive by the horns, I guide the antelope towards the vehicle and the waiting crate. Upon the horn pipes being applied, I feel safer and rather happy that I won't become a human sosatie on this afternoon. Once the Impala is crated, I turn my attention towards the vet ...

Without too much 'argie bargie' we arrive at a discounted amount for the afternoon exercise. The Impala is rather rumbustious inside the crate, but he settles down for the road trip to his waiting harem ... a lucky boy is our ram, in more ways than one!

22

NYALA RABBITS

Nyala are beautiful bushveld creatures! The bulls are stately and stand strong, with spiral horns and crisp white hair extensions when on parade. A cross between a kudu and a bushbuck ... Nyala are impressive animals and both male and females are exceptionally gifted with wild beauty! This species is easily tamed and Nyala make for great viewing at tourism establishments. Guests can comfortably observe these handsome antelope from the comfort of their lodgings.

Around the time of 'The Great Game Swindle', Nyala were fetching astronomical prices on auctions throughout the country. Every auction worth its salt had parcels of passively captured Nyala available. These parcels of wildlife were an auctioneer's dream, bids were fast paced and plentiful! After the sale, the transportation of the animals was easily affected with wildlife adapted trailers. Nyala represented an easy and lucrative wildlife ranching option. These antelope are prolific breeders, are easy to train over feed and their capture and transportation requirements complete the easy equation. They make for stunning photographic imagery and present well at catalogue game sales, either on large format print or digital screens. However ... the seller needs to supply the exact animal on offer ... or absolute clones of the animal represented in the catalogue! When you are paying twenty thousand rand per breeding cow ... Then that's what you, as a buyer, will expect to receive! Correctly so.

'Mr Black' starts appearing at a few of my auctions. I note his backbench attendance and how he records the lot numbers, prices achieved, buyer numbers etc. On the third occasion of his presence, he approaches me to discuss the possibility of supplying animals to my auctions in conjunction to out of hand sales. I agree to visit his property and in due course, we are joined in a symbiotic relationship. Mr Black supplies animals at short notice, when a capture is incomplete and this backup facility works well … for both of us.

On a particular auction, Mr Black secures a large entry of Nyala cows onto the catalogue - all these animals are touted as passively caught Nyala! On the day of the sale, the punters fall over themselves, throwing cash at the lots, 'smash 'n grab buying!' After the sale, I ask Mr Black how many Nyala cows there are on his property … Mr Black assures me … "Daar's baie." We get to work, delivering animals that were bought on the sale. Over time, I start to notice the breeding ages of the delivered animals decreases and the productivity of the investments are questionable. However, the buyers remain willing, as they are happy to be receiving Nyala females!

We have one last trailer load of Nyala to dispatch. It's a Friday afternoon and I'm ready to wrap up a long week, on a positive note! The logistics plan has been agreed upon and I have arranged to meet with the vehicle delivering the animals.

Murphy's Law … the driver is late, no communication! I wait and try to raise Mr Black. The phone just rings, unanswered. The hours tick by, slowly! The sun starts to retreat into the late afternoon sky, shadows drawing elongated, charcoal stretch marks onto the ground. The buyer is a little concerned, I am, more than that, I am shitting myself - there's a great deal at stake here! "Where the hell is this driver?" My call is finally answered by Mr Black ... "He's on his way." ... *Click*. He cuts the conversation short while I enquire as to the ages and general health of the animals loaded. The sun is dipping out of sight when I notice the utility vehicle and trailer barrelling up the long, corrugated stretch of gravel road. The trailer is bouncing over the irregular road surface, the tires getting grip on the secondary mounds of dirt. I watch the dust trail spewing from the speeding combination of vehicle and trailer tyres - the dust hangs high in the evening air, growing into a genie-like shape behind the speeding carrier.

As the driver pulls up next to me, he starts with the charm! All smiles and what a beautiful afternoon it is etc. I have no faith in this deflection tactic. My gut feeling is overpowering me; I need to see these animals on the trailer! (I can't afford any discrepancies) before the party gets properly broken! It's halfway broken, as it is.

I ask the driver to open the top hatches, so as to inspect the Nyala before we offload into the gathering dusk. The driver's phone starts to deliver its ringtone and he takes the call, I am a nuisance to him at this point. Mr Black is ripping into him; I make out the burble as it swarms past his earlobe into the evening air ... With that he hurries around the front end of the trailer and releases the bolt, opening the holding compartment to the outside world. A few seconds pass and a Nyala cow explores the open space with her large ears and wet black nose. Her large pear-shaped ears pivot forward, mimicking a forward listening station, quizzing the new environment. She gathers her hindquarters beneath herself and half lopes out of the trailer, landing squarely on the ground. She nudges slowly into the claustrophobic twilight, the gloom enveloping her shape as she moves off.

Everyone starts to relax a little and another mature cow steps gingerly out of the dark trailer, turning to look at us as she feels the new found ground beneath her hooves.

'The Kraut' is all about - "JA, JA, is gut JA ..." I'm not so sure, the shit is coming ... I think to myself.

While the driver and The Kraut are scratching each other's backs ... I see three more Nyala descend from the trailer in rapid succession! *BAM, BAM, BAM* and they are off. These last three animals conclude the delivery. Under normal circumstances this would ignite smiles and congratulations all around. Not this time ... the last three animals put distance between us and them, employing miniature strides! These aren't just immature females, they are babies! "Bloody hell man!" This is exactly what I feared would happen. The pieces of the puzzle start to fall into place for me ... The objective was clearly to deliver these animals in the dark and then to disown the stock in the light of the next day.

The Kraut is a little confused. To be expected, I suppose. He bid on mature breeding cows not lambs. "JA, JA, ve talk in ze morning JA?" Here we go ...

Psychopaths take some time to put their true colours on display Mr Black was about to exhibit a rainbow shower of colour!

The following days were nothing but interesting! The Kraut placed a restriction on his funds in the trust account. Mr Black wanted payment! No amount of persuasion would convince him of the error at hand. Besides the threat of law from The Kraut, all sorts of retribution was being laid at my door from Mr Black. A psychotic mind works in mysterious ways. In the end, I salvaged my relationship with the buyer and secured top prices for other animals he wished to liquidate. As for Mr Black … I never heard from him again.

23

AN ERROR OF JUDGEMENT

"Your honour, may I suggest a recusal at this point? The witness is unfit to continue." These words floated across the Grahamstown High Court as I addressed Judge, 'Gin & Tonic'. The witness box was occupied by my erstwhile client, 'The Shape Shifter' (also referred to as Shifty). This chameleon of a person lay slumped to the left, unable to lift his gaze towards the good judge as he responded (rather economically) under my cross examination.

Bullets of perspiration popped freely from the rapidly expanding and contracting pores on either side of his temples. Beach balls of sweat birthed themselves, some quicker than others. They joined the fore-running globules of guilt, before they traced a riverine path down the bulbous, flushed cheeks and creases in this individual's bull of a neck. Mental anguish taxed his brain and central nervous system. He attempted to navigate his way around and over the tightening noose of direct enquiry. Ultimately Shape Shifter was unable to answer, engage or physically present himself in this High Court trial. I suggested the recusal to Judge 'Gin & Tonic' out of compassion, departing from the business at hand - 'advocate' Hutchinson had left the building.

Now you may ask how does a layman, off the street, act as an advocate in a High Court trial? Shifty had sought advice on some colour variant Blesbok running amongst his common blesbok herd. I took one look at these colour rich creatures and suggested he place them on the upcoming Seven Fountains species - specific sale of blesbok. Shifty declined my marketing advice and requested an 'on the veld' price - net of capture, marketing, mortalities and transport costs. I was dismayed. How was I to arrive at a global figure for a ninety strong herd of common blesbok inclusive of a few colour variants, the likes of which I had never seen? On top of this, the capture area was littered with rocky outcrops, stands of vegetation and lay on a thirty-five degree slope ... "I don't know what these animals are worth, but I know they are worth money!" With this line of assessment, I hoped Shifty would place these colour variants and common Blesbok on the upcoming sale. It was not to be, he insisted on his first letter of engagement. I deliberated over this acquisition for two full days before committing to an offer in writing for the entire herd. I offered double the market rate for blesbok at the time. Shifty was over the moon, double the value for doing nothing and for no risk! I proceeded with the marketing for this blesbok auction, returning numerous occasions to photograph the animals. The marketing material would be top class! During the coming weeks I lit up the internet, WhatsApp, sms and all cell numbers on our database with pics, messages and verbal invites. I implored everyone out there to attend the first ever blesbok species-specific auction!

The auction is an absolute success with the top blesbok ram achieving one million rand, common blesbok close at an average of six thousand rand a piece. Unheard of prices for a common plains game species. An invitation lot of Black Impala sell for five hundred fifty thousand rand each. Yet, my invited buyer from the cradle of mankind did not advance on a single lot and was conspicuous in his absence from the big table. I met up with 'Mr Orange' at the bar, "There was just nothing that caught my eye," he said. I arranged to meet with him the next a.m., I wanted to show him my newly acquired blesbok. Making it known they were not for sale. I had placed the common blesbok on the sale and they had gone well. My plan was to retain the colour variants and breed these genes, for my own enjoyment. Mr Orange's telephoto lens was in aperture heaven, his eye glued to the viewfinder and his index finger played a slot machine symphony on the image trigger! I gently reminded him the animals were not for sale. When we reached the farm gate, he suggested a breeding programme inclusive of a magnificent colour variant ram he owned up north. I agreed and all parties concerned were excited about this new breeding venture and the heads of agreement that were signed. In the meantime, Shifty enquired as to how the blesbok sale had gone and I told him of the high prices achieved. "Well, at least you made some bucks," he said ... Auctions create market prices and yours truly had just converted every 'maplotter' and blesbok keeper into an 'Oligarch' 'cos you know ... every single blazed buck was now worth ... millions.

With prior notification, we set about darting blesbok at Shifty's camp. He attended the capture and observed proceedings from within his vehicle, parked at a premium vantage point. The French TV channel, Channel Five, filmed the capture. They also filmed the blesbok auction, as the crew were doing a piece on alternative business investments. Once we had darted a couple of the colour variants and a ram, they were loaded into the transport truck and sedated. Shifty climbed on top of the truck and looked into the holding compartments. Shifty had completed his right to inspection and the capture entourage left the property. We did not dart all the colour variants - leaving an ewe and her lamb. Darting this animal would have been unethical and unnecessary. I would capture the two upon my return for the balance of the herd. Dr Slick, the veterinarian in attendance, welcomed the decision and concurred we were acting in the best interest of the mother and her lamb. The bush telegraph morphed into Radio Africa and blesbok 'folklore' grew as long as the shadows cast by Gum trees in the late afternoon.

As I pen this piece, I can only speculate as to how Shifty arrived at his point of departure, departure from our deal, departure from his moral compass and departure from the truth. In due course I received a call from Shifty - enraged by the 'discovery' of colour variant blesbok missing from his property! ... Clearly they were missing after they were darted and removed by ourselves ... With Shifty in attendance. The call resulted in him cancelling the deal and forbidding my return to the property. Not long after this, the ewe and the lamb that were left behind, were advertised on OLX ... Go figure!

Hutchinson was now properly 'up the creek' my breeding deal was in tatters, the blesbok sold on the auction would not be delivered and capture costs for part of the colour variant package had been incurred. After pondering this situation for a few days, I sought counsel with 'The Bullfrog' a lawyer of purported standing. Without instruction, his assistant issued summons for capture of the balance of the herd at Shifty's property or one million rand. Shifty approached 'The Mole' and in the final hour for response, the battle lines were drawn, with a counter action to the value of six hundred twenty-five thousand rand. Needless to say, legal bills were the order of the day. Bullfrog considered this an open and shut case. However, between Bullfrog and his advocate, my purse was liquidated and I refrained from paying anymore of his relentless invoices. Bullfrog withdrew and disappeared faster than a warthog down an ant bear excavation.

The matter is set down on the roll in the Grahamstown High Court and there's no turning back. Advocate 'Aardwolf' and counsellor Mole arrive to represent Shifty. I arrive on my ace! I have no legal representation, save my knowledge of events, conviction in regards to my first prayer and the naive assumption that justice will prevail. After all, I have the written exchange regarding the deal, phone records and surely a witness that won't deviate from the truth under oath ...?

Judge Gin & Tonic presides and asks me as to where my legal representative might be? Shifty and his cohort stifle a giggle. These two clearly expect me to retreat, claiming no representation. They couldn't have been more misguided. Lawyer or no lawyer ... Shifty was going to answer for his actions!

Aardvark and Mole are jovial and light hearted. Aardvark and Judge Gin & Tonic are well acquainted in this house of law and verge on familiarity in their legal speak exchange. Judge Gin & Tonic seems to be a man of virtue and duly enquiries as to whether I am aware of the potential folly of continuing unrepresented?

I elect to continue.

I am allowed to start proceedings and I call Shifty to the witness box, it literally is a box. He takes his seat and at first looks rather brave. I note that his shirt collar and suit are a little ill-fitting. The high end of his shirt collar imprints into his neck, this rim of material would later soak up the sweat globules and represent a drowning Albatross around his neck.

The usual affirmations are confirmed - name, occupation, place of residence, relationship to myself and then I get the show on the road! Now Aardwolf is an advocate of note! He employs a mode of cross questioning that will flush out any uncertain facts from his witness. I have knowledge of his prowess and I intend to clone his skill set today! I will exercise a negative connotation in reverse to confirm a positive response for use against the incumbent witness. Another legal eagle of the Grahamstown's law fraternity coached me in this regard ... forewarned is forearmed.

Shifty answers my stock questions without much hesitation. I build his confidence and create an abundance of relief within his legal camp ... Pretty much like the Zulu King enchanted Piet Retief and his wagoneers ... It was time! I flicked the switch, engaging Aardwolf's technique and ripped the rug of confidence out from under Shifty's arse. The employment of Aardwolf's interrogation technique combined with his speech mannerisms, ripped into Shifty's barrel of guilt. The effect was immediate, exposing his uncertainty, forcing him to think in top gear, protecting statements that could not be amended once uttered. Aardwolf immediately recognised his own skill set besieging his client. He kicked out repeatedly at the table legs supporting his 'file factory'. His right shin bore the brunt of his frustration and fury! Shifty wilted under the sociopathic defiling of his prepared testimony. His ship was going down. His cohort shifted nervously on her bench, eyes wide shut, as I weaved her position of affiliation into the negative or positive line of cross examination. Was she - wasn't she an accomplice in this cluster fuck? Shifty became spent, unable to look up at Judge Gin & Tonic as he raspingly whispered inaudible responses to my questioning. Slumped sideways, eyes half cast to the floor timbers, with involuntary trembling racking his body. "You will look at the judge when you answer a question in this court," my voice carried forth, not overbearing but definitive in its command. Shifty was incapable of presenting himself. Surely I had achieved the moment of truth? When a witness cannot respond for fear of incrimination, does that not indicate perilous exhaustion of a prepared testimony? More so there was acute stress that manifested itself as the Judge perused the purchase and sale document for the animals in question. Shifty had denied all previous knowledge of this document during my cross examination. The good Judge was not impressed.

I could no longer lay waste to this fellow and called for the recusal. Gin & Tonic graciously afforded Shifty the escape hatch. He and his cohort were shepherded out of the High Court onto the pavement by Aardwolf and Mole. The pair of legals were not convinced they were on the winning team anymore. I could hear Aardwolf berating Shifty enquiring as to the correctness of his brief.

On Judge Gin & Tonic's exit from the chair, the court clerks rushed up to me, shaking my hand, proclaiming: "You got this." A transcript of this court case is housed in archives in Grahamstown.

Upon my taking the stand, I sense Aardwolf is tentative and unsure as to his approach, how is he to combat a clone of psychique and persona. The good judge is ready, pen in hand. Before I begin to answer Aardwolf I look up at Gin & Tonic and respectfully inform him that I will speak slowly allowing him time to connect pen to paper correctly, as I will extrapolate on each of Aardwolf's upcoming questions. My interaction with Gin & Tonic irritates the advocate and he lets me glimpse a crack in his facade. I bat his questions with confident conviction and leave him with no other option than … "No further questions your honour," I suspect he had cause to save the judge from writer's cramp, as the early questioning resulted in a concise explanation of how a Blesbok physiological system reacts to immobilisation chemicals.

Day two, and I know Aardwolf and Mole are charging Shifty like wounded buffalos! Closing arguments are presented. Aardwolf and Mole have regrouped and put on display a trolley full of dusty old case file ledgers and reams of other reference material. The advocate leads the charge and Mole concurs or cautions on the different lines of attack that Aardwolf seeks to destroy my personage with. I am cited as despicable and mercenary in my lack of 'fiduciary responsibility' towards my erstwhile client. Aardwolf is clutching at straws! That horse has a headless rider and anyway, Shifty euthanized this equine charge with his earlier testimony. Nevertheless, the advocate continues his assault and I am gobsmacked when he attempts to justify his client's apparent lack of recollection as to matters in question. All the while, smiling and nodding at the Judge, "Absolute snot," I thought.

My closing argument was not a patch on my earlier performance. I implored the good judge to take all the evidence, and the manner of testimonies into account and do the right thing - allow me access to capture my animals ...

I can only imagine the tortuous, complex wrangling that must have gone on post-trial! The outcome of this case would have far reaching effects on the legal system if I won ... After two weeks, the judge hands down a ruling in Shifty's favour ... I AM TO RETURN THE CAPTURED ANIMALS WITHIN TWO WEEKS.

Clearly, there was no aptitude regarding the information I supplied during my testimony ... It is not advisable to dart game in the height of summer - the animals internal organs may cook as the blesbok loses the ability to regulate its own body temperature. Besides this, relocation of game outside of the capture season, at the height of summer is deemed a criminal activity in the Government Gazette. I called Judge Gin & Tonic out on this judgement. He assumed the position of Pontias Pilot and washed his hands of it all. He suggested I engage with the opposite legal team. Mole had no issue with the animals being returned in the first week of capture season. I hoped reason would prevail - I was wrong. Shifty insisted on the ruling being upheld. Why would he insist on putting these animals' lives in jeopardy?

I refused to comply but sought another legal practitioner's input. Enter 'Humpty Dumpty'. Grahamstown is a small place and he had obviously heard of my high court escapades. However, he reviewed the communication from Mole insisting, in the first instance that I return the animals forthwith or pay Shifty six hundred twenty-five thousand rand. Humpty Dumpty suggested I comply with the order ... I refused. A rather vulgar Afrikaans expletive escaped his rounded maw of a mouth - Poes! He cursed aloud and threw his spectacles against the wall ... "Hutch, it says ... return the animals, it does not read, return the animals alive!" I borrowed the five thousand rand to pay for this legal advice and handed the future to the gods. Intel comes to me on the wind - Judge Gin & Tonic had ruled in Shifty's favour based on one technicality. I had no irrefutable proof that Shifty had inspected the animals on the truck before we departed. The net result of this sequence of events was my eventual sequestration. My bank accounts were frozen, assets sold off and on the day that my vehicle was repossessed, I stood in High Street, Grahamstown - penniless, left with just the clothes on my back.

My last conversation with Obelix went like this ... "Hutch, we will go for a coffee when you can afford it."

MY PERSPECTIVE
UNDERSTANDING THE BID

Every seller waits in anticipation for their stock to move up the roll and step into the ring. The auctioneer should start the bid slightly above market value, looking for the lucky strike! Remember, an auctioneer needs to preserve his voice - endless calling of ill-related values is a waste of the market's time and buyers' intelligence. This action will most certainly diminish the auctioneers perceived ability and professional standing. The opening bid is usually directed at certain buyers, the opening bid call is not a random - 'calling all pockets' exercise! A good auctioneer will have earmarked certain lots for the interest of relevant buyers. The increment levels that a good auctioneer implements, will find life, as the interest in the lot is stimulated. The bid becomes akin to a length of elastic, expanding and contracting with the increasing or diminishing interest. Extending the life of the elasticised bid is the auctioneer's prime objective! For while the bid lives, so does the financial advantage. With no advantage, there is no growth. He will massage and coax the bid, keeping the money pot boiling for as long as it is sustainable. As the demand slows or the number of buyers dissipate or lose interest, so too will the auctioneers bid value. The final bids will be worked very closely between the last of the punters. The final amount that a buyer is prepared to pay, is the moment his 'hand' is revealed. Strong buyers will at times, slightly overpay on opening lots, so as to flex financial muscle and put other buyers on the back foot or cause confusion in the market. Some buyers may even leave the auction, as they perceive the market to be above their mantlepiece ... My advice is simple. Never leave an auction early! Stay until the last lot.

In the final phase of the bid, the auctioneer will squeeze the last two bidders - each buyer will be aware of their financial Commitment in terms of the lot on offer. Fear of loss will be cross referencing these two players as they dance to the auctioneer's tune! Neither of the bidders will want to relinquish the lot. Via the diminished bid value, the buyers are lured, higher and higher in the monetary stakes. On top of the last two buyers 'mental mathing' each other, the auctioneer may employ a third force as he calls in a bid from a planted buyer. This will either drive the bid upwards or result in one of the buyers' financial 'hand' becoming exposed, forcing closure of his bid. When this happens, it would be prudent of the auctioneer to withdraw the planted buyer and collapse the bid on the last man standing unless the house is buying ...

Continuity and fluency of the bid commentary is imperative. If an auctioneer starts and stops the bid, this is a clear indication of few or no bids. It may also be that a buyer's ring has formed against the auctioneer. The inconsistent bid call will deter other buyers from entering the bid. This creates a dangerous situation for both auctioneer and seller. Bid spotters are used to gather in bids that the auctioneer might have missed. These gentlemen of the floor are vocal and their cries of Yiiiip! - Yesss! Or whistles, bring electricity to the atmosphere and add to the excitement of the lot on offer.

If you are an auction 'rookie' it is hard not to be drawn into the razzmatazz. Razzmatazz is exactly what it is! Bid spotters are very determined agents of the auction house and can appear to bully buyers into bidding on a lot ... and sometimes on 'a lot'!!

A buyer's budget can be left in tatters under sustained pressure from the auctioneer, bid spotters and of course ... Buyer 99! Creating value is the name of the game and very often the buyer operates in injury time!

Working the crowd and stroking egos is a large aspect of the auctioneer's ambit.

Most buyers will have a seven day payment facility with the auction house. This is basically free money! Think about that for a minute ...

Risk runs real for the auctioneer! The buyer might die, the stock might be lost in transit, the buyer might just disappear. There is an endless list of possible scenarios, included in the above is the threat of non-payment. On top of this, stolen stock placed on the auction can be a nightmare for the unwitting auctioneer! Stock thieves are everywhere and the easiest way to liquidate or launder stolen animals is through an abattoir or ... an auction yard.

My perspective. The auctioneer will attempt to achieve the highest possible price for the seller. The seller is the first point of care for the auctioneer. Buyers need to understand, the auctioneer is not your friend.

MY PERSPECTIVE
THE AUCTIONEER

There is a difference between an employed auctioneer and a self- employed auctioneer! The latter deals with all aspects of dispersal, whether it be equipment, livestock, property, vehicles or wildlife. In terms of the mandate, the self-employed auctioneer attends to the holistic management and effective sale of the mandated goods. This auctioneer does not just pitch up, conduct the sale and disappear! This auctioneer completes the service cycle!

The term liquidate does not extend solely to bankruptcy. The word, liquidate refers rather to the action of creating financial relief to the seller by metamorphosis of the asset into currency. This brings about cash flow and liquidity. Lack of cash flow can severely hamper the growth or even survival of any business, especially production businesses, such as animal husbandry or crop planting. Fixed assets represent wealth, however, the wealth is realised through two actions - bank leverage or the sale of the asset. Everything has a value, determining that value is an entirely different story. Too often auctioneers are approached as a last resort, or 'get me out of jail' miracle workers. An auctioneer is often called upon by lawyers to liquidate a client's assets. This is a last resort tactic that creates negative connotations and causes loss of face, while creating ill feeling or bad impressions of the auctioneering industry.

The auctioneer that is self-employed has a vested interest in the entire process of achieving the greatest financial value, during the conversion of assets into cash process. The company's brand with the figurehead of the auctioneer is attached to the public image of the exercise. This guy has far greater responsibilities resting on his shoulders! The employed auctioneer hammers the gavel on the day, thereafter he gets paid his commission and walks away - the further logistics are not on his programme. He has no responsibility as to delivery or any other hiccups that may present themselves after the final knock of the gavel.

Once the values of the assets have been achieved, funds should be channelled through a lawyer's trust account. This is a valid form of protection for all parties, as long as the lawyer himself doesn't have his fingers in the cookie jar!

Time is money and all too often the auctioneer has to achieve the near impossible for the seller! The call to liquidate assets at short notice is never an easy operation, the auctioneer will always be mindful of achieving the necessary values! Too short a run up to auction day and the guy on the gavel would have had to make plan A, B and C! Counselling sellers as regards values is an important part of the liquidation process. Many times, the seller has over capitalised on the asset and is looking for the capital plus expenses to be retrieved! The other hidden factor that could suddenly emerge, is a bunch of creditors looking to hijack the funds off the auction or the actual assets themselves.

An auctioneer is a confident, people's person with the ability to persuade! Persuasion during the bid calling process only happens when the auctioneer has built a rapport with the prospective buyers, before the sale. Knowledge of the buyer is paramount to success on the day. Both the seller and the auctioneer will have 'a hard day at the office' if the auctioneer is not up to speed with the subject and has no prior relationships to attending buyers. Relationships are built on trust and service! An auctioneer is sometimes provided with 'insider' protection, whereby the auction house will have buyers planted amongst the crowd. These 'buyers' may bid until the reserve or offset price is achieved. Should the bid fall on the planted buyer ... well, then the auction house becomes the proud owner of that lot. This modus operandi is viewed as underhanded or manipulative by attending buyers and is generally not condoned.

As regards to livestock auctions ... There are many external influences that determine the bid. In some cases, these influential circumstances affecting the reserve price on the day, have been put into play many kilometres from the current lot under the hammer! On occasion the lot in question is not even up for sale ... The stock is just being run through the ring to be simulated as a market ready lot ... Yet they have been pre-sold to an upcountry feedlot! Buyer 99 feeds on these lots! Perception is everything and this plot creates the idea amongst buyers and sellers that there is a vast amount of stock on sale! This attracts clients, stimulates market prices and creates a rabid economy! The economy is bordering on false ... This puts ears on the individual buyer. Trying to compete against the auction house is like 'farting against thunder'.

The net effect is that the prices are massaged and the auction house secures more sellers with the promise of high prices. As the auction house secures more stock, they drive harder bargains and on sell the stock in volumes to feed lots and abattoirs. When the auction house starts buying on the floor ... The house has a fifteen to twenty per cent head start on any of the attending buyers! Seven per cent commission plus vat is the first consideration, the second consideration, is the weight loss factor! A livestock unit can lose up to ten per cent of its body mass while in transit to the auction. Add in the travel factor ... standing over in a stressful environment takes a further toll on the live body weight of the animal. Compound this weight loss over a number of animals and this represents large amounts of currency!

All of the above translate into volumes of cash flow and profit for the auction house. Weaner calves are a top end aspect of the livestock business. Buyer 99 gets busy!

The next 'flytrap' that awaits the sellers pocket is ... the

auctioneer's scale! If, by chance, this piece of equipment is not calibrated and it under weighs ... the seller loses.

Having in-house buyers operating at an auction does create a sense of false economies, however, the in-house buyers are only pushed as far as the market demand goes and the benchmark is set! Selling livestock on an auction creates a host of other industries that all feed off the stock that runs through the auctioneer's ring. Each of the industries feeding off the seller's production will have negotiated deals with each other and the auction house. The vital link between the producer and the balance of industries, including the retailer that ultimately supplies the consumer, is ... The Auctioneer! The seller farms the animals and the auctioneer farms the seller. The auctioneer looks after the seller's best interests and creates cash for the seller. The relationship between the seller and the auctioneer is important to both parties! The auctioneer will create a 'feel good factor' amongst buyers and sellers. Social responsibility does form part of the auctioneer's ambit of commitment to the community he serves. Social responsibility can become a two edged sword for the auctioneer. Stepping on toes, putting noses 'out of joint' and negotiating politics, plus social climbing are all linked to ingratiating the auctioneer into every pocket of the community. All of this revolves around the stock supplied by the seller! They say ... no farmer, no food ... I say, "No farmer, no life!"

When it comes to stud sales, it is a common practice for members of the breeding group to bid on each other's offering. They are supporting their common cause. A stud animal is prepared for auction! Very few stud book sellers will put animals onto an auction straight off the veld! Generally, all animals would have been screened by the breeding group to ensure a quality offering on the day. Misrepresentation is an unlikely scenario in cattle sales, however, when it comes to wildlife ... Buyers beware! Many factors can railroad an unwary buyer and up-end the best efforts of the auctioneer. Point of origin, pregnancy, age, capture myopathy and injuries sustained during capture and transport are all influencing factors for both buyer and auctioneer. The last aspect in consideration of purchase is possible misrepresentation of genetics. The auctioneer sells, according to the information supplied by the seller! In many cases the auctioneer is no more knowledgeable than the attending buyers.

My perspective. The auctioneer supplies a valuable service to producers and is a vital link in the supply chain. The methodology may appear 'clandestine' to the outsider, however, the auctioneer takes the risks to protect the seller and is exposed on all fronts!

MY PERSPECTIVE
RISK

Risk passes from the auctioneer to the buyer at the 'fall of the hampasses' from the auctioneer to the buyer at the 'fall of the hammer'. Risk is a very real threat in the four legged world. Physical damage and/or death become massive financial detractors, at the drop of a hat.

The auctioneer is exposed to risk the minute the stock arrives at the auction yard. This threat intensifies for the duration of the presentation time that the lot is contained in the auction ring. Risk is a manifestation of loss of life, financial sabotage through unpaid bids and seller's misrepresentation! Reputation is the key pillar holding the auction house up. This can be brought down by psychotic sellers and rogue buyers! The only 'lick and promise' that glues everyone together is the livestock! The livestock promise is the constant, they are what they are. Humans are another ball game.

My perspective. The auctioneer is exposed on all fronts - risk presents itself in financial, criminal, intellectual and ethical means. Auctioneering is a lucrative yet hazardous occupation.

Note! - Loose goods ... Don't bite, kick, jump ... or run away! True story ... The final knock ... Operating as an auctioneer in the Eastern Cape was exciting and most certainly adventurous. Would I do it again ...? Possibly not ...

www.ingramcontent.com/pod-product-compliance
Lightning Source LLC
Chambersburg PA
CBHW031338060726
47590CB00007B/2518